MAKE HOLY THESE GIFTS

Make Holy These Gifts

Enchantment and the Catholic Faith

JAMES AND EVELYN WHITEHEAD

A Crossroad Book
The Crossroad Publishing Company
Chestnut Ridge, New York

Crossroad, Herder & Herder, and the crossed C logo/colophon are registered trademarks of The Crossroad Publishing Company.

Book design by the HK Scriptorium

Library of Congress Cataloging-in-Publication Data available
from the Library of Congress.

ISBN 978-0-8245-5045-5
Epub ISBN : 978-0-8245-5046-2

Books published by The Crossroad Publishing Company may be purchased at special quantity discount rates for classes and institutional use. For information, please email sales@crossroadpublishing.com.

Be bishops who are able to enchant and instruct.
Pope Francis to newly consecrated bishops

Much of poetry, music and the arts aims to "enchant"—and we must never strip that word of its aura of magical summons . . ."
George Steiner, *Real Presences*

Contents

Part Three: Imagination Enchanted

What in the World Is Enchantment?

Be bishops who can enchant and instruct.

Pope Francis

A PPEALING TO NEW BISHOPS to become enchanters, the pope further encouraged them, "Take care of your priests so that they may reawaken such enchantment with God in their people." And he reminded these new leaders, "It is joy that draws, that enchants, that enraptures. Without joy, Christianity deteriorates into exhaustion, pure exhaustion."[1] Many a bishop must have blinked at this invocation of enchantment, a term long associated with incantation and magical spells. They might well have asked along with this prologue: what in the world is enchantment?

From the beginning, Jews and Christians have come across events that fascinate and befuddle: bushes that burn but are not burned up; a spring of fresh water appearing in the midst of the desert; Jesus, dead and risen, suddenly visible like a ghost on the seashore. The whole Bible is a cornucopia of enchantment, "pressed down and flowing over" (Luke 6:38).

Catholics speak of this enchantment in the metaphor of sacrament. At any moment a most ordinary part of life might be transformed into something extraordinary. Water,

1

bread, sexuality are all blessed with this potential for epiphanies and transfigurations of every kind. "Nothing, [Annie] Dillard claims, could be more Catholic than a notion of God 'blazing from within' the created world."[2] Created by God, the world shimmers with holiness.

We are charmed and captivated by the rich *givenness*, this more than we could expect, more than we can account for. Creation itself intimates an abiding enchantment, "the dimly held awareness of something beyond and beneath the everyday, something hinted at in the daily flicker of loving moments or in the artist's struggle toward completion."[3] This sense of something "beyond and beneath" does not depreciate the everyday as deficient or somehow falling short of the real thing; instead this awareness appreciates—that is, adds value—rendering the ordinary yet more precious.

The enchantment of the world—its extravagant charm—summons us, awaiting our response. Once summoned, we in turn summon up enchantment in art, literature, and religious rituals. This summoning lies at the heart of religious faith. To believe in a Holy Spirit—invisible yet animating—is an exercise in ghostly enchantment. To envisage the cross-generational procession of humankind toward God as "a communion of saints" is a feat of imagination and a blessed enchantment. To believe in the possibility of "redeeming the time" (Ephesians 5:16) is to envision our unfolding lives as governed by more than fate.

Venues of Enchantment

A desert floor, arid and barren, suffers a sudden downpour of rain, and plants emerge from nowhere and bloom their hearts out. We know this is not magical; this is simply part of nature. Yet it is marvelous. We encounter enchantment throughout nature—an enchanted garden, a dark but inviting forest, the sigh of a rainbow at the end of a frightening storm. The world seems stocked with marvels and delights meant to dazzle us and, in so doing, restore our vitality. Author Annie Dillard is an apostle of nature's charm. "Our life is a faint tracing on the surface of mystery . . . we must somehow take a wider view, look at the whole landscape, really see it, and describe what's going on here." She concludes, "The universe is not made in jest but in solemn incomprehensible earnest. By a power that is unfathomably secret, and holy, and fleet. There is nothing to be done about it, but ignore it, or see." [4]

"Some enchanted evening . . ." We meet another person, often by chance, who has an immediate effect on us. Small gestures and a captivating smile capture our attention in ways new and alarming. We are smitten. Roberto Unger names the charming distress that accompanies such enchantments. "The lover must suspend the defensive aloofness that marks so much of his experience in society. He must run the risk of being rebuffed or disappointed. He must expose himself to perilous emotion and ridiculous gesture." Unger suggests that such an enchantment "always has something of the miraculous. It is an act of grace devoid of condescension or resentment." [5] In Marilynne Robinson's novel *Gilead,* an old minister wonders at falling in love with a much younger woman: "That there should be a voice in the whole world, and that I should be the one to hear it, seemed to me then and seems to me now an unfathomable grace." [6] Both estimates of enchanting love end with grace; but we are giving away our story.

We are listening to a symphony, and suddenly we are crying. We do not know the source of these tears and have no name for the emotions surging through us. Literary critic George Steiner observes that music is "brimful of mean-

ing which will not translate into logical structures or verbal
expression . . . [evoking] resonances in our bodies at lev-
els deeper than will or consciousness." Art and literature
approach us as enchantments that enliven and enrich our
lives. Art shares with religion the potential to trigger "a root
impulse of the human spirit to explore possibilities of meaning and of truth that lie outside empirical seizure and proof."[7]

The enchantments of nature surround us; the charm of
love assaults us; then there is the summoning of enchantment by novelists and poets and liturgists. This capacity to
summon enchantment is the special focus of this book: how
art and ritual, religious worship and spiritual metaphors
fashion words and gestures until they provoke responses
that captivate and charm us. When we are enchanted we are
taken out of ourselves, transported to other vantage points
from which to appreciate what we have in creation. Elaine
Scarry describes the enchantment of beauty: "at the moment
we see something beautiful, we undergo a radical decenter-
ing . . . all the space formerly in the service of protecting,
guarding, advancing the self (or its 'prestige') is now free to
be in the service of something else."[8] Enchantment awakens
us to the extravagance and giftedness of our lives. We are
likely to experience such exuberance as blessing.

In each of these encounters—with nature or with another
person, with art and with religious ritual—there is an epiphany where we see something new or something more, and
this insight triggers a transfiguration: our world is enlarged
and we are enriched.

Shadows of Disenchantment

For many in today's world the charm has vanished from their
everyday lives. Love affairs have ended poorly; work with

little sense of creativity or purpose has drained enthusiasm from their days. A mood of disenchantment hovers over much of contemporary life. Modern science, when reducing mysteries to problems, seems to have demonstrated that the faith of our ancestors is little more than superstition. We no longer inhabit a welcoming cosmos but find ourselves on the margin of a universe that operates by its own laws of motion and energy, mindlessly hurtling through space toward its—and our—ultimate extinction.

Disenchantment names the disappointment that darkens a social reality that no longer shimmers with promise and delight. *What you see is what you get.* Helen Macdonald, who rediscovered enchantment in the ancient, fierce gaze of the hawk she was attempting to tame, describes the blinkered perspective in a world grown disenchanted. "We are very bad at scale. The things that live in the soil are too small to care about; climate change too large to imagine. We are bad at time too. We cannot remember what lived here before we did . . . nor can we imagine what will be different when we are dead."[9]

Catholic philosopher Charles Taylor describes this modern malaise: "Disenchantment is the dissolution of the 'enchanted' world, the world of spirits . . . of wood sprites and relics."[10] For 1,500 years the Christian tradition had grown and prospered in this cocoon of enchantment. Nearly all its infrastructure—heaven above and hell below, seraphim and cherubim, an abiding spirit named the Holy Ghost—had been developed in this long and long-ago era. How is Christian faith to retain or recover its essentially enchanted quality in an environment grown disenchanted?

In the midst of a disenchanted world, artists, writers, and religious believers search for a means of regaining a sense of enchantment. It will not be the enchantment of our ancestors, but some form of a "re-enchantment" of life and faith. Writing in the Catholic magazine *Commonweal*, Joseph Bottum suggests, "The goal of the church today must primarily be the re-enchantment of reality," alluding to "the essential God-hauntedness, the enchantment of the world." [11] This book joins this search.

What Enchantment Looks Like

In Alice McDermott's novel *The Ninth Hour*, Sister Jeanne was assigned the task of transporting small children to an orphanage, often directly from the funeral of a parent or from a law court. Without much training as a professional nurse, she was good at this delicate assignment. "Out on the street with her charges, Sister Jeanne would make the trip an enchantment for the trembling little ones, pulling sugar cubes from her deep pockets or leaning down to point out something, or someone, that would make them laugh." [12]

Laughter enchants. John Ames, the aging minister in Marilynne Robinson's *Gilead*, wonders at the laughter that both cleanses and renews the human spirit. He watches two young men laughing, and "it seemed beautiful to me." He muses, "it is an amazing thing to watch people laugh, the way it sort of takes them over." This natural human reflex causes him to "wonder what it is and where it comes from, and I wonder what it expends out of your system, so that you have to do it till you're done. . . ." [13]

Robinson's genius lies in her ability to conjure a human activity like laughter and see it first as utterly natural, then as deeply graceful. In this same novel John Ames looks back at the dizzying experience of falling in love and laughs. "At that point I began to suspect, as I have from time to time, that grace has a grand laughter in it." [14] When we are fortunate, laughter measures the enchanting presence of grace.

Two Pictures That Enchant

Enchantment is in the eye of the beholder. This beholder has had two pictures in his office for the past forty years. They assume the place that religious icons might have filled in a more devout writer. One is a painting; the other a photograph. I find I cannot finish looking at them.

The painting is an inexpensive print of three men on their knees scraping the floor of an apartment. They are shirtless and bent over their task. This painting, "the floor scrapers" or—more impressively—*Les raboteurs de parquet,* by Gustave Caillebotte (1848–1898), hangs in the Musée d'Orsay in Paris where I came upon it many years ago. As my companions glanced at it, then moved on to other rooms and more paintings, I found a bench and sat, entranced by I knew not what in this painting.

It is a realistic portrait of lower-class men hard at work. Their seminude torsos suggest sweaty effort. French society at that time did not approve of the painting, finding its depiction of workers to be vulgar. What is it that so appeals to me? I cannot say, only that it absorbs my attention.

The second picture in my office is a now-yellowing photo cut from a newspaper long ago. It is a photo by Dorothea Lange of a woman in winter coat and high heels walking down a street. She glances ever so slightly to the right, as though to check the small boy—her son?—who walks carefully, head down, two steps behind her. The child is placing his foot on the pavement, seemingly with great care, as he moves along. The woman does not remind me of my mother as much as the little boy—so earnestly following—reminds me of myself.

In the photo, as in the painting, I see something that charms me, that triggers a light that appears within, but without sufficient wattage to clearly illumine what it points to. I see and do not see. By both pictures I am held in minor wonderment and I am pleased. I cannot finish looking at them.

When we are enchanted we often cannot say how or why. Bruno Bettleheim, in *The Uses of Enchantment*, analyzes the force of fairy tales on children and argues that "the story's enchantment . . . depends to a considerable degree on the child not quite knowing why he is delighted by it."[15] This *not quite knowing* the source of wonder—the enigma and uncanniness woven through creation—is part of the charm of adult enchantment as well.

Sociologist Richard Jenkins hazards a definition of this curious experience: "Enchantment conjures up and is rooted in, understandings and experiences of the world in which there is more to life than the material, the visible or the explainable. . . ." Enchantment conjures up a world "in which the philosophies and principles of Reason or rationality cannot by definition dream of the totality of life. . . ."[16] This dream of wholeness, so different from an analyzed slice of life, economic, political or civic, speaks to distinctive yearnings in the human heart.

What Kind of World Is This?

We move from the question "what in the world is enchantment?" to the question whose focus shifts to the world itself. What kind of world is it that can spontaneously open onto epiphanies and transfigurations? What kind of world is it that allows for artistic expression and religious ritual that overthrow our settled ways, alerting us to richer, deeper ways to live? How has language itself become the chief enchanter, deploying metaphors that mean more than they say? What does enchantment tell us about the world we inhabit?

Richard Jenkins asks, what is "the place of enchant-ment—specifically spirituality, desire and playfulness—in whatever it is that we call human nature"?[17] In the follow-ing pages we will explore these three domains of what Jen-kins calls "the expressive dimensions" of life and their role in feeding "the capacity of humans to routinely resist and subvert" the forces of disenchantment.[18] One area where spirituality, desire, and play converge is music. Literary critic George Steiner muses on this curious domain. "Music and religious feeling have been virtually inseparable. It is in and through music that we are most immediately in the presence of the logically, of the verbally inexpressible but wholly palpable energy in being that communicates to our senses and to our reflection what little we can grasp of the naked wonder of life."[19]

The Sacramentality of the World

The Catholic genius lies in the recognition of the world as sacramental. An ordinary part of life may, at any moment, be transfigured into something extraordinary. The bread on the kitchen table can, when blessed and shared, become the spiritual nourishment for which we have long hungered. *Give us this day our daily bread.* Water, ordinary H^2O that washes off the day's grime, may be felt as a cool blessing. The aging minister in Marilynne Robinson's *Gilead* watches a young couple running, laughing, from a brief shower of water, and reflects, "It is easy to believe in such moments that water was made primarily for blessing, and only sec-ondarily for growing vegetables or doing the wash."[20] Bread, water, even vulnerable bodies joined in love become enchanting sacraments of the blessing that is creation.

Catholic writers strive to name this magical quality of

matter that renders the world enchanting. The poet Gerard Manley Hopkins envisioned "The world [as] charged with the grandeur of God."[21] Priest sociologist Andrew Greeley links the capacity for enchantment with the power of imagination. "The Catholic imagination . . . views the world and all that is in it as enchanted, haunted by the Holy Spirit and the presence of grace."[22]

The lame walk, the blind see, weapons are repurposed as farm implements. All this takes place only in a world that has become enchanted. Enchantment names the jolts in consciousness with which we register the epiphanies and transfigurations of the wonder all around us. Another name for this is grace.

Resources

1. The pope's call for the bishops to be enchanters is reported in the *National Catholic Reporter*'s blog the "Francis Chronicles," September 9, 2016. The article was accessed at ncronline.org/blogs/francis-chronicles/Pope-Francis-new-bishops. The previous year he had also invoked this metaphor, calling for the new bishops to encourage their priests to also enchant. This speech, dated September 10, 2015, was accessed at ZENIT.org/articles/pope-francis-address-to-new-bishops.

2. Annie Dillard is quoted in John Waldmeir's *Cathedrals of Bone: The Role of the Body in Contemporary Catholic Literature* (New York: Fordham University Press, 2009), 66.

3. Paul Lakeland, *The Wounded Angel: Fiction and the Religious Imagination* (Collegeville, MN: Liturgical Press, 2017), 12.

4. Annie Dillard, *Pilgrim at Tinker Creek* (New York: Harper-Collins, 1974), 11, 275.

5. Roberto Unger describes love in *Passion: An Essay on Personality* (New York: Free Press, 1984), 238 and 221.

6. Marilynne Robinson, *Gilead* (New York: Farrar, Straus and Giroux, 2001), 209.

7. George Steiner, *Real Presences* (Chicago: University of Chicago Press, 1989), 143, 271.

8. Elaine Scarry, *On Beauty and Being Just* (Princeton, NJ: Princeton University Press, 1999), 111.

9. Helen Macdonald, *H Is for Hawk* (New York: Grove, 2014), 265.

10. Charles Taylor, *A Secular Age* (Cambridge, MA: Harvard University Press, 2007), 553.

11. Joseph Bottum, "The Things We Share," *Commonweal*, August 23, 2013, https://www.commonwealmagazine.org.

12. Alice McDermott, *The Ninth Hour* (New York: Farrar, Straus and Giroux, 2017), 51.

13. Robinson, *Gilead*, 5.

14. Ibid., 207.

15. Bruno Bettelheim, *The Uses of Enchantment: The Meaning and Importance of Fairy Tales* (New York: Vintage Books, 1977), 18.

16. Richard Jenkins, "Disenchantment, Enchantment and Re-Enchantment: Max Weber at the Millennium," *Max Weber Studies* 1 (2000): 29.

17. Jenkins, "Disenchantment," 29.

18. Ibid., 14.

19. Literary critic George Steiner names the play of music as yet another human enterprise that induces enchantment. See his *Real Presences*, 217.

20. Robinson, *Gilead*, 28.

21. Gerard Manley Hopkins, "God's Grandeur," in *Major Works* (New York: Oxford University Press, 1986), 114.

22. Andrew Greeley, *The Catholic Imagination* (Berkeley, CA: University of California Press, 2001), 184.

Part One

The Christian Adventure

The Bible is a motherlode of enchantment, displayed in a dizzying array of epiphanies and transfigurations.

Christians have from the beginning fashioned rituals and ceremonies meant to summon God's grace in this broken world.

The enchantment of every life plays through the alternating current of presence and absence; abundance and scarcity; feasting and fasting.

Catholic novelists in the twentieth century often opposed the faux enchantments of the world and the genuine charm of their faith.

CHAPTER ONE

The Biblical Language of Enchantment

They heard the sound of the Lord God walking in the garden at the time of the evening breeze.

Genesis 3:8

ENCHANTMENT DEBUTS in the opening pages of the Book of Genesis: "So God blessed the seventh day and hallowed it" (2:3). This hallowing or "making holy" will be the signature of sacred enchantment throughout the Jewish and Christian heritage. A day at the end of the week, a meal at the close of the day, an ordinary wooden cross can be lifted up and made holy.

The Bible teems with enchantment from the original enchanted garden of Eden to the ghostly appearance of the risen Jesus to his startled disciples preparing breakfast on the shore; from the burning bush that befuddled Moses to the transfiguration of Jesus before his closest friends that caused them to stagger and mumble incoherently.

During the early centuries of Christian history, "enchantment" belonged to a family of phenomena—magic, spells, sorcery, soothsaying—that Christians found unsavory. The wonders wrought by their God would be described in terms of mighty deeds instead of any resort to the occult arts. Leviticus had warned against witchcraft (19:26). Deuteron-

15

omy produced a long list of forbidden practices, including soothsaying and the consulting of ghosts (18:10). The Second Book of Kings cautioned against seeking out wizards (21:6).

The New Testament ends with the command in the Book of Revelation to eschew sorcerers and pornographers (22:15). The Greek term for sorcerer is *pharmakoi*—pharmacists, those who concoct potions. The enduring concern about occult practices distracted Christians from employing the term *enchantment* to describe the captivating miracles and astounding transfigurations wrought by their God.

Enchanted Gardens

The biblical story of creation takes root in an idyllic, enchanted garden. The authors of this narrative had heard of "the hanging gardens of Babylon," one of the wonders of the ancient world; they likely knew of the *Epic of Gilgamesh* and the account of a "garden of the gods," aka Paradise.

This memory garden anchors the Christian imagination and its reckoning of how life had begun. For centuries this imaginative meditation on our origins was read as literal history, sparking from time to time the search for its geological site. Only with an increased awareness of the workings of evolution has this account been recognized for what it is: a wondrous mythic reconstruction of how it might have all begun. For some believers this realization seems to doom the story of the garden of Eden to mere fabrication. For many others, this story seems to get it about right: the luxurious charm of creation itself; the memory of some ancient disaster that left our species wounded and prone to violence; the hope of finding our way through difficult childbirth and sweaty work to a life of rest and delight with our creator.

The Bible returns to this image of a garden in the erotic story of lovers in the Song of Songs. An "enclosed garden" becomes the secret precinct of love for these lovers who would come to be interpreted as symbolizing the divine affection for us humans.

What is the peculiar appeal of a garden as an emblem of enchanted space? We can imagine our ancestors, millennia ago, in the midst of a desert trek coming suddenly upon an oasis. In an arid terrain there appeared a wholly other kind of place hosted by water, palm trees, and many plants, a place not of their doing. That first garden was all epiphany: nature's gift that set the human imagination humming with plans for similar sites, now crafted by humans. The appeal of land cordoned off from the wilderness with hedges and fences; a place where we bend nature to grow in tidy, weed-less rows: is this not part of its charm?

David Cooper, in *A Philosophy of Gardens*, suggests that the garden serves as a symbol of humans and nature cooperating to render a plot of land both fruitful and beautiful; what Cooper calls "a co-dependence of human existence and the 'deep ground' of the world and ourselves."[1] Grains and fruits grow according to their own mysterious dynamics, but we assist this natural process, erecting borders, inserting nutrients, and adding moisture. Gardens also witness to extravagance: plants and fruits gathered in abundance in a single site to feed our stomachs and delight our eyes. Literary critic Elaine Scarry suggests that "Gardens exist for the sake of being beautiful, and for the sake of having that beauty looked at, walked through, lingered in."[2]

The metaphor of garden endures in modern literature as a symbol of enchantment. Evelyn Waugh, in *Brideshead Revisited*, describes the excitement of falling in love: "I was in search of love in those days [hoping to find] that low door in the wall . . . which opened on an enclosed and enchanted garden."[3] Here the garden is necessarily hidden—"enclosed," reserved for lovers.

Thomas Merton turned this metaphor on its head with his description of his entry into the ascetical life of a Trappist monk. "Brother Matthew locked the gate behind me and I was enclosed in the four walls of my new freedom. And it was appropriate that the beginning of freedom should be as it was. For I entered a garden that was dead and stripped and bare."[4] Merton savored the paradox of a barren, wintry garden as the place he would seek his spiritual nourishment.

The image of garden rings some chime in the soul, even if our religious enchantment with a sacred garden is more anticipation of an ultimate reconciliation than nostalgia for an ancient loss. Marilynne Robinson, in her novel *Housekeeping*, writes of humans as transients in this world but not exiles. Aware that they do not finally belong here, humans journey toward a final communal resting place—"a garden where all of us as one will sleep in our mother Eve."[5] Whether history or hope, historical fact or myth, the garden at the beginning of Genesis continues to enchant.

A Burning Bush: Getting Moses's Attention

"The bush was burning but it was not consumed" (Exodus 3:2). The Book of Exodus tells the story about a budding relationship between God and Moses. The context is Yahweh's effort to capture Moses's attention. First, God makes a walking stick to be suddenly transformed into a snake, then just as quickly have it revert to being only a stick. Then Moses's hand is made leprous, and just as quickly returned to health. Having secured Moses's attention with these sleights of hand, Yahweh turns to the main event: the revelation of a covenant that God means to forge with the people of Israel.

At Horeb "the angel of the Lord appeared to him in a flame of fire out of a bush." Moses's curiosity was piqued. "I must turn aside and look at this great sight, and see why the bush is not burned up." God then calls Moses by name, granting him this revelation: "I am the God of your father." He is instructed to remove his sandals because he is standing on holy ground. "And Moses hid his face, for he was afraid to look at God" (Exodus 3:6). Moses is bewildered by this bush and the voice of God emanating from it; he is curious about this uncanny display, and he is charmed.

Blessings That Make Holy

The seventh day of creation is hallowed, made holy. The ground that Moses is standing on is made holy. At the heart of a life of faith are blessings that make holy everyday lives, ordinary time, humble bread and wine.

"The Lord bless you and keep you; the Lord make his light to shine upon you and be gracious to you; the Lord lift up his countenance and give you peace" (Numbers 6:24). Throughout the Bible the ancient Israelites recorded blessings experienced as "finding favor"—the scriptural name for grace. Abraham and Sarah, long past childbearing age, learn that they are to bear a child; they have been chosen to begin a race whose members will one day outnumber the grains of sand on the seashore. This unlikely gift of sexual fruitfulness is the shape of the blessing, the favor they have found with God.

When Ruth finds favor with Boaz, she lies down beside him on the threshing floor and "the Lord made her to conceive and bear a son" (Ruth 4:3). And this child, unlikely offspring of a non-Jewish widow, would be in the line of David that led to Jesus the Christ. This phrase, *finding favor*, appears throughout the Bible to name the blessings that God mysteriously sends to make us more fully alive. This is but one aspect of God's enchanting extravagance.

This story of blessing and grace appears in the New Testament account of Mary's pregnancy. Surprised by the new life within her, Mary learns that she has found favor with God. In Luke's Gospel this epiphany is messengered by an angel: "Blessed are you among women and blessed is the fruit of your womb" (Luke 1:42). Here, too, finding favor means fertility and new life.

The Greek word for "finding favor" that we meet throughout the Bible is *charis*, which also means gift or blessing. The enchantment imbedded in this word becomes apparent when we notice a similar word—*charismatic*. A gifted teacher charms a gathering with compelling stories and images. Charismatic leaders, almost by definition, are those who possess the ability to enchant. This linkage of charismatic leadership and blessings helps us make sense of Pope Francis calling new leaders "to be bishops who enchant and instruct."

Christian Enchantment: Power and Wonder

Somebody touched me. I felt power going out of me.
Luke 8:46

In the New Testament the word *dynamis* (power) appears more than a hundred times to name an uncanny energy that enlivens, bewilders, and heals. Perhaps the most enigmatic appearance is the story of a woman with a disabling condition who draws close to Jesus as he is moving down a crowded street. She reaches out to touch him. Jesus suddenly stops and demands, "Who touched me?" His companions assure him that many people had brushed past him in this crowded thoroughfare. But he countered, "I felt power going out of me." Jesus had not initiated this tactile encounter. He had not made a conscious decision to heal this woman of her affliction. A mysterious healing power had been drawn from him by her contact, seemingly without his own awareness. The enchanting epiphany in this story is about healing power and how it is made available when a person comes close enough to this extraordinary person.

In much of our contemporary world, power is seen as a possession: the judge or bishop or politician *has power*. As a possession of a few leaders, power will always be part of a zero-sum reality: another's power comes at our expense. And power is seen as a dangerous possession. Lord Acton had it right when he observed that "power tends to corrupt and absolute power corrupts absolutely."

In the New Testament we find a very different vision of power. *Dynamis*—the Greek word for power—is a *dynamic*, an energy that flows throughout the world. It is emphatically not a personal possession that someone—Jesus or a bishop or a judge—might dispense at will. It is a relational force, an energy that flows among persons, sometimes to injure, sometimes to heal.

This relational aspect of power is on display in the Gospel story of Jesus returning to his hometown. Here he finds that his former neighbors know him too well as the carpenter's son. They cannot imagine him as able to do anything for them. In such an environment Jesus finds that he cannot do any "mighty deed" (*dynamis*). Without some receptivity on their part, Jesus was left with little power to heal. Power as descriptive of human interaction brings it in touch with the enchantment of being intimately in touch with another.

In the everyday life of Christians, God's power is experienced both as charism and conscience. Believers become aware of some ability or skill—teaching, consoling, even negotiating—that they might use in service to others; this strength or charism is not of their doing; it has come as gift and a power to be shared. It is how they have found favor. And, if they are fortunate, they become attuned to the interior authority of conscience: their own maturing confidence in their judgments of how to respond to the questions and crises that life provides.

The Enchantment of Wonder

Jesus was a wonder-worker. But among all the itinerant wonder-workers of his time, Jesus's followers knew him as something different. Power and wonder intermingle in a number of stories about Jesus. Jesus seemingly has the power to calm a storm at sea, and his companions are astonished. The Greek term *thauma* (wonder, astonishment, amazement) describes the wondrous works that poured forth from Jesus under the force of the Spirit. Mark's Gospel describes Jesus's first public appearance. Entering a synagogue he began to preach. "They were astounded at his teaching, for he taught them as one having authority" (Mark 1:21). At another time when he is preaching, he is stopped by a heckler, a man demented. Jesus drives out the man's evil spirit, and "they were all amazed" (1:21).

In Matthew's Gospel we read the story of Jesus and his friends being caught in a storm at sea. His terrified disciples beg his help, and the storm dies down. "They were amazed, saying 'what sort of person is this, that even the winds and the sea obey him?'" (8:27). These uncanny actions were both wondrous and enchanting.

In this same chapter we find that Jesus himself can be

amazed. A soldier comes to Jesus to ask him to heal his daughter. When Jesus decides to visit the man's home to see the child, the soldier urges Jesus to use his power to simply heal the child. He sees Jesus as like himself, a person of authority who has only to give a command for it to be fulfilled. "When Jesus heard him, he was amazed and said to those who followed him, 'truly I tell you, in nowhere in Israel have I found such faith'" (Matthew 8:10).

Wonder and awe are emotions that arrest our attention, open our eyes to a dazzling creation, and serve as doors to the sacred. Wonder alerts us to boundaries in life where our sure knowledge wanes and our curiosity intensifies. Historian Caroline Walker Bynum names this emotion: "we wonder at what we cannot in any sense incorporate, consume or encompass in our mental categories."[6]

Wonder and enchantment are siblings. Each wrests our attention away from ourselves and opens us to other selves, other realities. Wonder and awe work as epiphanies that startle and enchant.

Epiphanies in the New Testament

In the New Testament, enchantment shimmers in stories of epiphanies and transfigurations. After Jesus died (and there was talk of his appearing to some disciples) his friends went back to earning their livelihood on the sea. One morning, coming to shore after a night of fishing, they made out a ghostly figure that looked familiar yet unsettling.

> Just after daybreak, Jesus stood on the beach; but the disciples did not know it was Jesus. . . . Jesus said to them, "come and have breakfast." Now none of the disciples dared ask him, "who are you?" because they knew it was the Lord. (John 21:4, 12)

The disciples knew and did not know who this was. It cannot be Jesus since he has died. But it appears to be the Lord. Here the uncanny is joined to enchantment, an appreciation of what we cannot comprehend, cannot get our heads around. In all the appearances of Jesus after his death and resurrection we encounter someone who is most real but no longer one of us. Jesus's presence in these scenes is always brief, little more than a glimpse. His is a real presence, if ghostly, beyond all our usual categories of how humans engage with one another.

We see this startling realization played out in the episode in Matthew's Gospel where Jesus is approached by a non-Jewish woman who pleads for him to heal her sick daughter. At first Jesus does not respond, does not know what to say. His friends urge him to send this bothersome woman away. Then he tells them what he had always assumed: "I was sent only to the lost sheep of the house of Israel" (Matthew 15:24). This seemed to be the limit of his vocation.

The woman, meanwhile, was not dissuaded but fell on her knees and asked again, "Lord, help me." Now Jesus seemed rattled and responded in an unkindly fashion. "It is not fair to take the children's food and throw it to the dogs." Not stymied by this insult, she pressed on, reminding Jesus that even dogs get scraps from their master's table. Jesus is astonished by her persistence and relents. "'Let it be done for you as you wish.' And her daughter was healed instantly." If we can see Jesus as coming to his vocation gradually—as we do—we may see this episode as a moment of epiphany for Jesus himself.

A Transfiguration

The most detailed and dramatic story of transfiguration occurs in the account of the disciples' sudden and staggering realization that Jesus is more than a holy man. We come across the account of the transfiguration as though it were a dream sequence. Ascending a mountain with Jesus, his three companions are suddenly struck dumb by a startling epiphany. The Gospel story is ornamented with the pyrotechnics of a mythic tale: they find themselves on a mountain (a place whose elevation allows further vision or revelation); Jesus's appearance is radiant, and his clothes turn dazzling white (signaling special illumination). He seems to be talking with ancient prophets.

His companions, staggered by this display, show signs of intense befuddlement. They enter a kind of stupor—the Greek word here is *hypnos,* as in hypnosis. Peter suggests that they set up tents, but his disorientation is signaled with the added remark, "not knowing what he was saying" (Luke 9:33). In the account in Matthew's Gospel we see more signs of confusion: "they fell on their faces and were filled with awe" (Matthew 17:6). Then when this dream-revelation comes to an end they suddenly see themselves with the Jesus with whom they are familiar. He is again their everyday companion; but now he is also much more, something they do not pretend to comprehend. This epiphany works a transfiguration in their recognition of Jesus as the son of God.

Epiphanies and Transfigurations in Everyday Life

"In Louisville, at the corner of Fourth and Walnut, in the center of the shopping district, I was suddenly overwhelmed with the realization that I loved all those people, that they were mine and I theirs." Thomas Merton, Trappist monk and prolific author, describes this startling epiphany of a reality that ordinarily remains out of sight. "It was like waking from a dream of separateness, of spurious self-isolation in a special world, the world of renunciation and supposed holiness. The whole illusion of a separate holy existence was a sham."[7]

This sudden, startling epiphany was also a transfiguration: the isolated world of the monk, safely separated from the world in the cocoon of the monastery, was seen "as a sham." Fifteen years earlier a withdrawal from the world had served Merton as he sought out "a small, secret colony of the Kingdom of God in this earth of exile."[8] This sacred isolation no longer served Merton as God was directing his attention and writing toward a broader, richer world. This transfiguration in Merton's life took him eventually to the international conference on world religions in Bangkok, where he died in 1968. His life trajectory, from isolated monk to someone engaged with the spiritual concerns of the whole world, also describes the shift for many Catholics in the 1960s and '70s whose careers were transformed from vocations in "religious life" to lives of service in the wider world.

In Marilynne Robinson's prize-winning novel *Gilead*, John Ames wonders at the rhythms of enchantment that seem to play through the world. "It has seemed to me sometimes as though the Lord breathes on this poor gray ember of Creation and it turns into radiance—for a moment or a year or the span of a life." Like the epiphanies throughout the Bible, such transfigurations are often gifts of the moment. Robinson continues, "And then it sinks back in itself again, and to look at it no one would know it had anything to do with fire, or light."[9] Such musings lead the aging minister to a larger reflection. "Wherever you turn your eyes the world can shine like transfiguration."[10]

Resources

1. See Donald Crawford's review, in *Notre Dame Philosophical Reviews,* of David Cooper's *A Philosophy of Gardens,* https://ndpr. nd.edu. The quotation from Cooper is found on p. 144; Crawford's online review is not paginated.

2. Elaine Scarry, *On Beauty and Being Just* (Princeton, NJ: Princeton University Press, 1999), 70.

3. Evelyn Waugh, *Brideshead Revisited* (New York: Little, Brown and Company, 1944), 31.

4. Thomas Merton, *Seven Storey Mountain* (New York: Harcourt, 1948), 410.

5. Marilynne Robinson, *Housekeeping* (New York: Farrar, Straus and Giroux, 1982), 192.

6. Caroline Walker Bynum, *Metamorphosis and Identity* (Cambridge, MA: MIT Press, 2001), 52.

7. Thomas Merton, *Conjectures of a Guilty Bystander* (New York: Doubleday, 1968), 145.

8. Merton, *Seven Storey Mountain,* 383.

9. Robinson, *Gilead,* 245.

10. Ibid., 245.

Chapter Two

Summoning Enchantment:
The Drama of Worship

Come, Holy Spirit, enlighten the hearts of your faithful and you will renew the face of the earth.

Psalm 104

Enchanting Gestures: An Altar Boy's Delight

"MASS WAS THE BALLET of my youth." Looking back at the spiritual aspirations of his youth, a man recalls the enchantment of the liturgy. Putting on the cassock, the young altar boy stepped into another world—"a world where your walking and turning were the peaceful glide of a sacred corpus, a world where your body was less visible but where your movement was more noticeable." He reflects how "the body can be a delight to the eye . . . it is part of a dance, an ancient and honorable choreography."

Serving at the Eucharist, "an altar boy's body became a stage prop. Even a young, shapeless youth could feel in his flesh that his movement was grand and dramatic. The bows, the genuflections, the well-timed turns, the subservient liturgy, all of these were part of a great sacred drama. They were something to see. And to the altar boy, they were something to feel."[1] In these memories and reveries the

28

sacred and the sensual intermingle; liturgy and enchantment embrace.

Summoning the Spirit

"Do this in memory of me" (Luke 22:19). We gather for the
liturgy on Sunday because we have been summoned. At
the heart of the Eucharistic liturgy, the celebrant, speaking in the community's name, summons the Spirit of God
to transform ordinary bread and wine into something yet
more nourishing. "Let your Spirit come upon these gifts to
make them holy, so that they may become for us the body
and blood of our Lord Jesus Christ." If this prayer is not
enchanting, nothing is. Sacraments are exercises in sacred
enchantment as we perform rituals and ceremonies, trust-
ing that ordinary elements in life—water, oil, bread—may
be transfigured into something extraordinary.

When we are charmed by another person, or captivated
by a scene in nature, or entranced by a poem, we are being
summoned to a new level of appreciation of life itself. A
woman, confronting a serious challenge, summons up
her courage; her courage is already on tap but now must
be evoked front and center. A man receives a summons to
appear in court; this is more than an invitation to drop by
when convenient. Many Christians experience a vocational
calling as a compelling summons. A summons often has an
edge of the imperative; it is an invitation with attitude.

At the beginning of the Jewish/Christian story, Abraham and Sarah were summoned to set out and dare life in
a new place. They were our first responders. Generations
later a woman named Hannah gave birth to a son whom she
would dedicate to God's service in the temple as the servant
of the priest Eli (1 Samuel 2:21, 26). One night, asleep in the
temple, Samuel thought he heard Eli calling him and rushed

to the elder priest's quarters. Eli assured him that he had not called Samuel. This exchange was repeated a second and then a third time until Eli realized that it was the Lord who was summoning Samuel. He tells Samuel, "Go, lie down; if he calls you, you shall say, 'speak, Lord, for your servant is listening.'" In our own lives God often needs a number of summonses in order to finally gain our attention.

Jeremiah is summoned to become a prophet of the Lord. "Now the word of the Lord came to me, saying, 'before I formed you in the womb I knew you. And before you were born I consecrated you'" (Jeremiah 1:4). Jeremiah resisted manfully: "Truly, I do not know how to speak, for I am only a boy." God rejects his excuse. "Do not say, 'I am only a boy.' For you shall go to all to whom I send you." The summons is relentless. "Gird up your loins; stand up and tell them everything that I command you" (Jeremiah 1:17). This summoning continues in the New Testament as St. Paul begins his letter to the Christians in Rome by recalling that he has been "summoned to serve as apostle" (Romans 1:1).

Literary critic George Steiner writes of "the summons of creation" and traces the link between summons and enchantment: "much of poetry, music and the arts aims to 'enchant'—and we must never strip that word of its aura of magical summons. . . ."[2] For Steiner, language itself can serve like an "annunciation of a 'terrible beauty' or gravity breaking into the small house of our cautionary being." He appeals to this scriptural *annunciation*—the summons of Mary to her vocation—to capture something of the enchantment that art and literature can produce. "If we have heard rightly the wingbeat and provocation of that visit, the house is no longer habitable in quite the same way as it was before."[3] There will be summonses that change our life.

The summons that Steiner finds in creation itself, and especially in literature and music, is both inviting and confusing. "We are creatures at once vexed and consoled by summons of a freedom just out of reach. . . ."[4] Again, Steiner: "That which comes to call on us—that idiom, we saw, connotes both a spontaneous visitation and summons—will very often do so unbidden. Even where there is a readiness, as in the concert hall, in the museum, in the moment of chosen reading, the true entrance into us will not occur by an act of will."[5]

Enchantment Lost and Found

Many Catholics recall Vatican II as a summons: a calling of the church into a more daring embrace of the modern world. *Aggiornamento*—updating—was the pope's name for this summons. But the liturgical reform that ushered in the vernacular in place of the traditional Latin seemed to some a loss of enchantment. Robert Royal, in *A Deeper Vision: Catholic Intellectual Tradition in the Twentieth Century*, expresses his disappointment at "the loss of mystery and elevation," and concludes, "ours is not a great era for exalted language. Much of the English Mass oscillates between the banal and the maudlin." For some Catholics the sonorous rhythms of liturgical Latin—the *mea culpa, mea culpa, mea maxima culpa*—carried an enchantment now sadly missing in the liturgy. Royal objects to what he sees as "the shallow rationality of the new vernacular" that for him is associated with "modern anti-Christian culture and middle-class mores."[6]

Royal's case against English in the liturgy echoes the consensus of the pious women in Mary Gordon's novel *The Company of Women*. These women who gathered regularly to hear the Latin Mass offered by Father Cyprian, their favorite priest, lamented recent liturgical changes. Charlotte, one of their number, summarized their objection. "'There's nothing like a Latin mass, I always say.' 'English is not a spiritual

language,' Father Cyprian added, 'It's the language of mer-
chants.'"[7]

* * * *

*The scene: a small gathering of Catholics outside a church in Rome
in the year 350 of the common era. The group appears disgruntled.
They have come from the celebration of the Eucharist where, for
the first time, the language of the liturgy had been changed from
Greek to Latin. Church leaders had explained the shift: few people
in the Roman Empire these days spoke Greek, which meant it was
difficult for many worshipers to follow the prayers of the liturgy.
But this new form of prayer, admittedly in their own language,
felt uncomfortable. They were accustomed to the sacred sounds
of Greek in the Mass and other liturgies. Greek, they grumbled,
is, after all, the language of the Scriptures themselves. They had
always heard Jesus's words spoken in Greek at the liturgy. Hearing
the opening words of St. John's Gospel, "in the beginning was the
Word," they had relished hearing the Greek term Logos—Christ as
God's Logos/Word that made sense of the world—the very logic
of the universe. But at the liturgy they had just attended they
heard the Word of God spoken of as the* Verbum. *This Latin term
emitted no sense of the sacred, no nuance of enchantment. Latin
was, after all, the language of the street, the chatter they heard all
around them, the speech of pagans.*

* * * *

Royal objects as well to the turning of the altar to face the
community. He acknowledges that Romano Guardini, one
of his heroes from the 1950s, did on occasion turn "around
the altar and put the students in a semi-circle," but "the
intention was never to create community—still less to make

community a central focus." Royal appears yet more vexed when thinking of this reorientation of the altar, "where the priest is facing, not God, as in the old form, but the congregation. . . ." [8] The choice appears to be facing God or the community.

Royal's objections remind us that liturgical enchantment arises, in part, from aesthetic considerations: the interior darkness of the church during centuries without electricity became in time itself a symbol of mystery and enchantment; candles, once ordinary sources of light, in time became themselves holy objects; the liturgy performed in a foreign tongue added a hint of the exotic and the exceptional.

Halls of Enchantment

1950. My older sister leading the way, our family of four arrives for Sunday Mass at St. Francis de Sales parish in Moorhead, Minnesota. A finger in the holy water font; a quickly made sign of the cross. As we approached an empty pew we looked up at the altar, which was raised three steps above the floor of the church. Three tall candles flanked the golden tabernacle where the Blessed Sacrament was reserved. On each side in front of these candles were candelabra with smaller candles. The red sanctuary lamp burned just to the right of the altar. Above all this, the very large crucifix dominated the scene.

I recall being shushed into silence by my mother as we came into this sacred space. I remember my mother lighting a votive candle and praying for her uncle who had a problem with alcohol. I remember the statues of Mary and Joseph that filled the side altars like guardian icons.

The enchanting heart of the Mass occurred when the priest bent over the host and said the Latin words *Hoc est enim corpus meum,* and raised the host that had at that instant become the body of Christ. It was astonishing that a priest could do this.

In 1950 we were enchanted by the sacred silence of the church, and often the somber darkness of this holy place. Each of us alone together before God. We were enchanted by the Latin prayers, bells ringing at strategic moments, the incense and monstrance so prominent in the ceremony of Benediction. We were enchanted by the realization that Christ was overwhelmingly present here even if he had been forgotten in the secular world beyond this hall of enchantment.

2020. Seventy years later and I am sitting in the chapel where we now attend Mass each Sunday. At the center of this large circular space is a simple wooden table. It stands on the floor; no steps to climb. There is no tabernacle on the table; no candles. The table is bare. No statues, no votive candles. No altar railing separates us from this table. The sanctuary lamp burns in a side corner of the space, out of sight for many of us. Newcomers might be disoriented by this circular, crucifix-free space: Where are they to look? Which way do they turn to face God?

The celebrant enters, and the Eucharistic liturgy begins with energetic singing and biblical readings in English by lay leaders. The reading of the gospel and homily follow. During the "prayers of the faithful," my mind goes back to my mother kneeling before the votive candles making similar petitions. Then a woman wearing a long white robe enters and sets the bare table with a white cloth. She then brings in special vessels with hosts, then cups with red wine. The celebrant approaches the table and, among many prayers, speaks in our name the *epiclesis*—the summoning of the Spirit to descend on this bread and wine and transform them into the nourishing body of Christ. Hearing these words in English we know this transfiguration can only be the work the Spirit, not the celebrant.

This is the same Eucharist that I fondly remember from my youth, yet the sense of enchantment has shifted. In 2020 we are enchanted not by a high altar as site of the Holy Sacrifice of the Mass, but by the ordinary table being set for our sacred meal. We are enchanted not by a sense of Christ's guaranteed presence in the tabernacle but by the growing sense of God's presence as friends, neighbors, and others filter into this worship space. At the kiss of peace—an ancient tradition we did not have in my youth—we greet the regulars around us and visitors as well with handshakes, nods, and, with some, fervent hugs. This lovely, motley crew has been summoned to become the Body of Christ on this day in this place: enchantment enough.

The Liturgy of the World

> *How oddly holiness situated itself among the things of the world, how endlessly creation wrenched and strained under the burden of its own significance.*[9]

Christian worship stages, again and again, the drama of salvation: the story of the surprising blessings that appear, epiphany-like, to transfigure our lives. In rituals of fellowship, nourishment, and forgiveness, these sacred ceremonies summon the enchantment that has always already been awaiting us throughout creation. Karl Rahner reminds us, "We gather together in worship not because our lives are devoid of grace but because we need to express all the grace-filled moments of our lives, which are so easily overlooked or ignored." What we celebrate in worship is not something that does not occur in the everyday events of our ordinary lives. What we celebrate is "the innermost, ever-present endowment of the world with the absolute mystery of God." This is what Rahner calls "the liturgy of the world."[10]

The liturgy of the world is human history itself with the unending interplay of God's grace and human lives broken and blessed. Specific liturgies offered by the church are symbolic distillations and enactments of this cosmic enchantment. When, in the 1800s, a scientific worldview began to replace an earlier naïve vision of an enchanted world, Catholic theologians erected a firewall between "nature," which appeared to be subject to its own laws of motion and energy, and the spiritual world of God's grace (the supernatural realm). A two-storey world evolved, with grace stationed above and beyond "nature." Grace could be imparted to this natural world but the transmission would be through the church's sacraments. Settling into this defensive posture over against an unbelieving world, the church began to think of its own worship as the one and only liturgy. In a disenchanted world the church would provide enchanting liturgies as Catholics would "gather together hoping to meet God who seems so impossible to find in our everyday world."[11]

In the last century, Christians have come to realize that there exists no place called "nature" that is separate from God's gracious presence. All creation is saturated with the grace of God. Pierre Teilhard de Chardin was keenly aware of this *liturgy of the world* when he offered his "Mass of the World" while on an anthropological dig in northern China. "Since once again, Lord . . . I have neither bread, nor wine, nor altar, I will raise myself beyond these symbols, up to the pure majesty of the real itself; I, your priest, will make the whole earth my altar and on it will offer to you all the labors and sufferings of the world."[12] Rahner summarizes the conviction of his fellow Jesuit, Teilhard: "The experience of God is primarily to be found hidden in the midst of ordinary life, in our experiences of hope, responsibility, love and death."[13]

The liturgical summoning of enchantment is on special display in the weeks leading up to Easter. Christians struggle—going against the cultural grain—to enchant the ordinary weeks of late winter and early spring with new meaning and focus in the days of Lent: a season of slowing the pace of life and paying new attention to the deeper aspirations of our hearts. At the beginning of this season the church offers a ritual of blessing with ashes. In this ironic benediction foreheads are brushed with a smudge of ash, recalling the biblical memory of "ashes to ashes, dust to dust." Here the ordinary meaning of ashes as dirt is transfigured into ashes as reminders of our mortality and the paradoxical promise of life beyond these humble cinders.

As the season of Lent reaches its climax Christians gather for a Good Friday liturgy. At the center of the assembly is placed a large wooden cross. Each person comes forward to touch with reverence this wood, which is embedded with memories of Christ's suffering and our gratitude for the gift of his life. In this expression of reverence, the cross—ordinary wood—is transfigured and enchanted.

The Easter Vigil itself, with its dramatic lighting of a fire in the darkness outside the church building, with the passage of new fire from the large Easter candle to the small candles held by participants and a procession that illumines a darkened church, is the centerpiece of Christians' expression of an enchanted world. The sacred ceremonies of the liturgy transfigure ordinary things—bread and wine, but also ashes and wooden crosses—with new and extraordinary meaning.

This Matter of Blessing

John Ames is distressed. The aging minister in Marilynne Robinson's *Gilead* has failed to find reconciliation with his godson, Jack Boughton.[14] As Jack prepares to leave home yet again—and likely for the last time—Ames asks a favor. "The thing I would like, actually, is to bless you." Jack, the non-believer, shrugged and replied, "What would that involve?" Ames answers: "Well, as I envisage it, it would involve my placing my hand on your brow and asking the protection of God for you." When Jack consents, the old minister recalls, "I did bless him to the limits of my powers."

God has blessed us with life, with the nourishment of friends and lovers, with purpose and direction for our lives. Blessing, making holy, appears to be God's job description. Eventually we get the point: we too are meant to bless. And so we bless our newborns, those who are marrying, those approaching death. All this only makes sense if we already find ourselves in a world enchanted by God's presence.

We bless water to make it special for sacred liturgies and call it "holy water." Sitting down with friends and family to a meal we take a moment to "bless" the food. *"Bless us, O Lord, and these your gifts which we are about to receive from your bounty through Christ our Lord."* In this brief ritual we suspend our usual flow of thoughts and words to recall how this sustenance has come to us, through many hands, to nourish and delight. The hope in this moment of blessing is that we become more attentive to the blessings of creation that feed every part of our lives. We do not pray that the food be altered, but that we may be.

Last Mothers' Day in our faith community, the celebrant asked all the mothers in the gathering to stand. These persons stood for a moment in silent recognition by the larger community. Then the celebrant asked the rest of the gathering to stand, extend their right hands and together offer a blessing on these mothers. An older Catholic might wonder: When were lay persons granted the ability to bless anything or anyone? Is this not the job of the ordained? The communal blessing we participated in that day was a ritual expression of gratitude to these members of the gathering. These mothers, so recognized in a public fashion, were likely to feel the pleasure of being singled out. In this brief exercise they were finding favor, being thanked for their generous lives. The community felt blessed by their many contributions, and on this special day all experienced a blessing.

Appendix: The Play of Ritual

As the day comes to an end in Shanghai, two events begin to unfold—one private, one public. In one part of this great metropolis, a woman stands silently in a small park located between two apartment buildings. Gradually she begins to move her body slowly through a series of careful, precise gestures. One leg is drawn in, then extended as she carefully pivots on the opposite foot. Her arms move gracefully, accompanying the movements in her torso. Undistracted by others who are passing by, she is intensely focused in her practice of *tai ji chuan*. Visiting teachers in Shanghai, we are enchanted by the concentrated flow of her actions. We may guess that her focus has, at least on some days, ushered her into a mood of enchantment.

Far across the city a theater company readies for its dramatic presentation of the evening. Actors check their costumes and practice the lines of their scripts. Scenery is arranged on the stage. Soon the curtain will go up, and, once again, the actors will perform an oft-told tale, made alive again tonight in this theater. When the drama is well performed the audience will likely find it charming.

Each of these performances is an intentional action, executed with care and focus. Each is repeated day after day, the same gestures enacted again and again. The bodily movements in each instance are stylized. These actions are neither random nor spontaneous but carefully rehearsed behavior, performed for a precise purpose. In these energetic practices people are summoning enchantment.

Liturgies of worship come to life in the play of ritual. For much of the twentieth century, ritual developed a bad reputation as mindless, even compulsive repetition. In recent decades scholars of every type have been rediscovering the richness of ritual. Rituals serve as a body language, deploying physical movement and carefully rehearsed gestures to perform what is difficult to put into words. Liturgist Edward Foley defines ritual as "patterned, shared, public behavior, expressing a meaning and purpose that cannot be put into words alone, in the face of some reality larger than ourselves." [15]

Scholars today emphasize the breadth of ritual and ceremony: "promises, commitments, excuses, pleas, compliments, pacts—these and so much more are ceremonies or they are nothing. It is thus in the medium of ceremony that the peculiarly human part of life is lived."[16] Sociologist Emile Durkheim caught the transformation that ritual effects, moving individuals out of their private selves into communal concerns. "It is in the effervescence of ritual that the individual concerns of daily life are transcended and society is born."[17] Rituals, then, are symbolic activities that lie at the very core of both culture and religion. Ceremonies are a central strategy that both cultural and religious traditions deploy to celebrate, to bless, and to enchant their shared life.

Resources

1. John Shekleton, "Homosexuality and the Priesthood," *Commonweal*, November 22, 1996, 17.

2. Steiner, *Real Presences*, 139.

3. Ibid., 143.

4. Ibid., 153.

5. Ibid., 179.

6. Robert Royal, *A Deeper Vision: Catholic Intellectual Tradition in the Twentieth Century* (San Francisco: Ignatius Press, 2015), 25, 198.

7. Mary Gordon, *The Company of Women* (New York: Ballantine, 1980), 175.

8. Royal, *Deeper Vision*, 224, 137.

9. Marilynne Robinson, *Home* (New York: Farrar, Straus and Giroux, 2008), 102.

10. Michael Skelly, *The Liturgy of the World: Karl Rahner's Theology of Worship* (Collegeville, MN: Liturgical Press, 1991), 18–19, 86.

11. Ibid., 75.

12. Thomas King, "The Mass on the World," Appendix I, *Teilhard's Mass: Approaches to "The Mass on the World"* (New York: Paulist Press, 2005), 145.

13. Skelly, *Liturgy of the World*, 18.

14. Robinson, *Gilead*, 241.

15. Edward Foley, *Ritual Music: Studies in Liturgical Musicology* (Collegeville, MN: Liturgical Press, 1996), 115.

16. Herbert Fingarette, *Confucius: The Secular as Sacred* (San Francisco: HarperSanFrancisco, 1972), 7, 14.

17. Emile Durkheim's definition of ritual is quoted in Robert Bellah and Steven Tipton, *The Robert Bellah Reader* (Durham, NC: Duke University Press, 2006), 151, 164.

CHAPTER THREE

Rhythms of Revelation

A little while and you will no longer see me; and again a little while and you will see me.

John 16:19

THE CHRISTIAN SCRIPTURES witness to the alternating current that runs through every life: presence and absence; abundance and scarcity; feasting and fasting. The repeated, uncanny shifting of these poles—from delight to dismay to delight—evokes its own kind of enchantment.

Presence and Absence

Throughout the Hebrew Bible, the ancient Israelites were repeatedly made aware of a presence (*shekinah*), bewildering yet engaging, that was leading them from slavery in Egypt to a new life in "a land flowing with milk and honey." This presence stirred the tent in their desert encampment where Moses met with God. This presence made itself felt in the cloud that hovered over this encampment; when the cloud moved it was time for the Israelites to set out again on their journey. In this early period of their courtship with God the Israelites found in nature—a bush, a cloud, a rustling of wind on the flap of a tent—proof of God's inviting, protective presence. The theme of a tent of visitation would con-

tinue into the New Testament, where John's Gospel begins
with the memory that the Word "has pitched its tent among
us" (John 1:4).

The epiphanies and transfigurations that flood the New
Testament are testimony to a peculiar kind of presence:
a presence most real but unlike other ways we are present to one another. This is a presence we cannot produce
but can await in faith; it is a presence most mysterious and
enchanting.

In the New Testament, Jesus embodied this presence of
God among us, captured in the name *Emmanuel—God with
us*. And after his death and resurrection, the Holy Spirit
would take up the role of mysterious, charming presence.

* * * *

*God of Israel, God of Jesus, your name is Shekinah, Presence. We
feel your saving presence in our bodies, our emotions, our hopes.
You appear in deserts and oases, in crises and at quiet meals. Your
epiphanies calm our fears and heal our shame. Help us to recognize
you in all your faces—in the flesh as well as in the spirit, in Eros
as well as in Logos. Help us remember that Jesus is God's desire
in the flesh, God's body language. Make us alive to our world, and
through it, alert to your presence.*

* * * *

In the many biblical stories of God's presence, we meet
again and again the curious theme of God's absence. The
sterile environment of the desert—its lack of water, food,
shelter—served as a mysterious backlighting to reveal the
presence of their God. The exile in Babylon was experienced as a traumatic absence of their city and temple, yet
from it came the impulse to assemble the Torah, God's
word made portable to cherish in every future diaspora

and exile. The revelation of these stories is that presence walks in absence. For humans, there is no such thing as a guaranteed sense of divine presence, just as we are never perfectly present and attuned to one another. God's gracious presence in history will always be an epiphany, a presence that appears with surprising illumination out of apparent absence.

Two disciples were returning to their village after witnessing the devastating events of Jesus's death (Luke 24). Disconsolate as they walked toward Emmaus, they were joined on the road by a stranger who asked the cause of their sorrow. Then he spoke to them, recalling Yahweh's promise of life that is born of death. His words relieved their hearts, and they urged him to join their evening meal. As the story tells us, "in the breaking of the bread" they recognized the stranger as Jesus. Then, as suddenly as he had appeared to them, Jesus vanished. The flash of this epiphany—this momentary glimpse of Jesus who comes in the guise of a stranger—did not leave them empty or discontent. Instead, their spirits were revived: "Were not our hearts burning within us!" From this day Christians were meant to see strangers in a new light; this was to be an ever-repeated epiphany.

Generous Absence

The celebration of Pentecost is the high feast of presence and absence for Christians. The disciples gathered in an upper, empty room, keenly aware of Jesus's absence. They had had glimpses of him since his death and believed that he was somehow still among them, but that day this thin memory offered little consolation. For a time they had enjoyed his engaging presence, but now it seemed they were left with only memories. In this domestic desert, they did not know where to turn. Without his guidance what were they to do? Glancing around the room looking for leadership, they were looking only at themselves. In their newly disenchanted world, where were they to turn?

Then in a commotion they could not explain, that we cannot explain, they experienced a wind or breath or spirit that forcefully uplifted them. Jesus's confidence and hope somehow came alive again for them. Discouragement gave way to a new enthusiasm. They left the room to tell others the good news that suddenly seemed urgently important. Hearers reported that their energy was audible in their words, which made sense even to those who did not speak their language.

Looking back, they could see that Jesus's absence that day was generous. Were he still with them, they would have had the luxury of depending utterly on him. Without him, they had to look within, to summon their own conviction. Hesitant followers had to fill this painful, generous absence with their own initiative.

This generous absence is built into every community. In a certain parish, a priest works with three lay women in a shared ministry. He is talented and able to encourage and support the women who work with him. Then one day he falls ill and must be absent for several months. At first, the women panic; what to do without their capable, priestly leader? Then, at first hesitantly, they assume his role and complete many of his tasks. They are surprised to realize they are up to it. They find in themselves a confidence and even skills they had not anticipated. In the space that the priest's good works had formerly so amply filled, their own gifts blossomed. His absence generously opened a place for their own abilities to come to life.

* * * *

*Since I have lost all taste for life, I will give free rein to my com-
plaints; I shall let my embittered soul speak out (the Book of Job).
My soul thirsts for you; my body aches for you like a dry and
weary land (Psalm 63). God of presence, help us to bear your mysterious absence. Help us through the darkness of the nights when
we cannot see you, the discontent of winters when we cannot feel
you, the sorrow of seasons when we cannot hear you. Attune us to
the absence that is generous—emptying us of a cherished past in
preparation for your surprising future. Lead us not into despair,
but toward the hope of your coming.*

* * * *

The Enigma of Abundance and Scarcity

A large crowd had come to listen to Jesus. The day was
late, and they were in a deserted spot—a scarcity of both
time and resources. When Jesus tells his friends to feed
the people, they complain that they have only a few loaves
of bread and some fish. Jesus tells them to go through the
crowd and gather what they could find. When they return,
Jesus blessed these resources, and the food is distributed
and—amazingly—there turns out to be more than enough
to feed the entire group. "All ate and were filled. What was
left over was gathered up, twelve baskets of broken pieces"
(Luke 9:19).

This is a parable of scarcity and abundance: an abundance
of people nourished despite a seeming scarcity of resources.
Was this a one-off event, a miracle that only Jesus, the son of
God, could accomplish? Or is there, perhaps, a larger message here: resources held in private and kept out of circulation will always mean a scarcity in the larger community.

Jesus turns fragmented resources and privately held sustenance into bountiful nourishment. By sharing their meager amount of food the people seem to multiply it; breaking their bread, they made more of it. Apparent scarcity obscures a hidden abundance.

Enchantment arises out of wondrous aspects of creation—a sonata or landscape or new friendship—that escapes our full understanding or control. Enchantment arises as well in the paradoxes that mark our existence. One of these is the almost magical appearance of abundance out of what had seemed to be intractable scarcity.

"I have come so they may have life, and have it in abundance" (John 10:10). The Gospels recount again and again the interplay of scarcity and abundance. The core account of Jesus's message of abundance—his feeding the multitudes—appears five times in the Synoptic Gospels. The story itself is multiplied, emphasizing the point of abundance.

The Invention of Scarcity

Scarcity, of course, is often genuine: the poverty that afflicts so much of the world, the enduring lack of strength that accompanies a long illness, our inability to solve problems within our own family. Scarcity can be very real and most painful.

Often, however, scarcity is more apparent than real. Another town lacks food, and our storerooms are full. Or becoming depressed, we are convinced that we have no friends, while these very persons gather at our gate, waiting to be readmitted to our life. Scarcity may be not only apparent but fabricated: a human invention and an intentional practice. The expensive watch retains its value only if it remains scarce; the status associated with a luxury automobile is diminished if too many people obtain one. Consumerism trains us in an economy of necessary scarcity.

The church, led by fallible humans, falls prey to the temptation to create scarcity. When the church decides that lay persons cannot preach at a Eucharistic service, it depreciates these gifts and manufactures scarcity. When liturgical leadership is restricted to unmarried men, we all but guarantee that the sacraments will be in short supply. This fabrication of scarcity reached its apex in the historical declaration that "there is no salvation outside the church." The church now had the franchise on salvation, ensuring it would be made scarce.

But Christians, in their better moments, recognize the gifts that flourish among them. Taking advantage of these charisms and talents, a community of faith recovers a God-given abundance. In Jesus Christ, God has given us great abundance. We, the church, continue to invent scarcity. And yet clues and hints abound in this world of scarcity of God's abundant, even extravagant gifts.

God's Extravagance

The Gospels overflow with parables of extravagance and excess. A tiny seed sprouts into a gigantic tree; a few seeds scattered on good ground multiply, not twofold or tenfold, but a hundredfold (Mark 4:8). A wayward son, having wasted much of his inheritance, is welcomed home by his father in a display of extravagant affection. Workers who are hired in the final hour of the day receive a full day's wages. This generosity evoked grumbling from those who had worked the entire day: "These last have worked only one hour and you have made them equal to us who have borne the burden of the day and the scorching heat" (Matthew

20:12). But the master replied to those who were looking for just treatment, "Are you envious because I am generous?"

In all of these parables, the revelation is not about doing things properly or in good measure but about an excessively generous response. The message seems to be that we do not receive what we deserve (thanks be to God!). Instead, we are loved excessively by our God and receive blessings we neither merit nor can account for.

"Give and it will be given to you." At first, this advice seems to reinforce the logic of equivalence, of a *quid pro quo*. But Jesus adds, "a good measure, pressed down, shaken together, running over, will be put in your lap" (Luke 6:38). Generosity will not to be repaid in equal portion, but in excess, "running over." This Gospel statement calls to mind a ritual celebrated in many cultures: wine is poured into a small ceremonial cup until it overflows—not in error, but with intent. An observer—especially a Western observer— might well rush forward, urging the pourer to stop. "Don't waste the wine! You will stain the table." But the point of the ceremony is to demonstrate excess and extravagance. Such rituals celebrate blessings that overflow the small cups of our lives. Linking these two memories, we might say that our God is a creator who does not know when to stop pouring.

Jesus's parables of extravagance are echoed by Paul's vocabulary of excess. Paul uses the same Greek word, *perisseuein*, twenty-two times to express God's extravagance. In his letter to the Ephesians, he writes of "the riches of his grace that God has *lavished* on us" (1:8). To the Philippians he offers, "This is my prayer, that your love may *overflow*" (1:9). In 1 Thessalonians, he prays, "May the Lord make you increase and *abound* in love for one another" (3:12). Lavish, overflow, abound: these are all efforts to translate the single

Greek word that Paul repeatedly used to express God's extravagant grace. Theologian David Ford describes these passages as examples of Paul's "rhetoric of abundance . . . the pervasive sense of a lavish generosity in blessing, loving, revealing, and reconciling."[1]

The Dance of Feasting and Fasting

On this mountain for all peoples, Yahweh Sabaoth is preparing a banquet of rich food, a feast of fine wines. (Isaiah 25)

The experiences of feasting and fasting are celebrated in every culture, as banquets and harvest festivals alternate with seasons of drought and hardship. The Jewish and Christian traditions have placed great importance on this alternating current of human life. The prophet Isaiah is the patron saint of the feast, as he summons the image of the final banquet that God has planned for us.

The New Testament records the many festivals and banquets that Jesus attended. These include both the wedding feast at Cana and the meal at which a woman intrudes to pour expensive fragrant oil over Jesus's head. In other stories, Jesus spoke about positions of honor at the banquet table and of inviting people "from the highways and byways" to participate in the feast.

These celebrations were so frequent that the people around Jesus took notice. Impressed by the ascetical lifestyle of John the Baptist, they voiced their concern: "John's disciples are always fasting and saying prayers, and the disciples of the Pharisees, too, but your disciples eat and drink" (Luke 5). Jesus's reply pointed to a rhythm built into life: "You cannot make wedding guests fast while the bridegroom is still with them, can you? The day will come when the bridegroom will be taken away from them, and then they will fast in those days" (Luke 5:33–35).

In the early centuries of Christianity, fasting became a regular and sometime extreme practice in monastic life. Feasting fell out of fashion as a religious discipline, Christians judging that "the time to fast" had arrived. Gradually the Eucharistic banquet commemorating Jesus's final meal with his friends evolved into a highly restrained ritual, and the weekly celebration eventually became known as "a day of obligation." The ideal of virginity and the later discipline of celibacy attached to priesthood in the Western church prescribed a strict fast from sexual activity "for those who would be perfect." In Christian life today, we are returning to a deeper appreciation of the rhythms of feasting and fasting.

Welcome to the Feast

We feast both to celebrate and give thanks. In harvest festivals, we recognize survival and bounty. When we feast, we do more than simply take in nourishment; we make a celebration in our nourishment. We bring out candles, a special tablecloth, the good wine. If the food satisfies our nutritional needs, feasting nourishes other famished aspects of our lives—especially our hunger for community and delight. Festivals and carnivals testify that the human spirit needs regularly to indulge. Without the occasional feast, our souls begin to starve.

At its best, feasting is a disciplined performance. A banquet proceeds at a leisurely pace, making "fast food" seem out of place. Since a major portion of our delight comes in sharing the occasion with those we love, we rarely feast alone. A feast is not an orgy; we do not abandon ourselves to food or drink or sex. Genuine feasting, in fact, teaches us to avoid excess. When it degenerates into a display of mindless abandon or conspicuous consumption, a party fails as a feast.

The Christian liturgy offers the example of a holy feast. We prepare colorful vestments and banners, add incense and song, and celebrate in unison our blessings. Along with other feasts, liturgical celebrations—when not reduced to repetitive or empty gestures—instruct us in an important truth: feasting is a communal art, not a private indulgence.

We feast not just with food and drink but with all our senses. Listening to a symphony or attending an opera provides a feast for the soul; a hot bath is a more humble but no less sensual feast for the body. At a museum, we feast our eyes on art that others have created. But plagued by the busyness of our lives, we may fail to feast. Weighed down with work and worry, we insist we have no time for such luxuries. But eventually, deprived of this nourishment, our souls begin to wither.

Welcome to the Fast

The delights and discipline of feasting find their complement in fasting. Fasting has often been seen as an exercise reserved for monks, nuns, and other religious elites, but not for ordinary folks. Today, we are returning to the celebration of fasting as an ordinary discipline, part of every life.

In the contemporary retrieval of fasting as a healthy discipline, we find a richer motivation. Fasting is not meant as a repudiation of the body and its passions, nor should it spring from a desire to punish a guilty soul. Fasting is an exercise of concentration, not deprivation.

Unavoidably, a rush of duty fills our lives; each day overflows with demands of what has to be done. These demands are often good in themselves, but their insistence crowds out other hopes and dreams. To fast is to rest briefly, in the midst of busy lives, in order to attune our hearts to neglected possibilities. In fasting we interrupt the ordinary rhythm in our life, so that we may listen to other longings. Fasting practices us in paying attention, so that we may be more present to our heart's desires.

As Christians return to the experience, we recognize how strangely nourishing a period of fast can be. Interrupting the ordinary rhythms of our lives makes us more alert, more awake. This may be rooted in the physiology of fasting: jolted by a lack of food, the body goes on alert. But getting past the initial alarm, we come to appreciate the emptiness—in spirit as much as in body. Those who fast report their senses are sharpened and their minds less distracted, as the overwhelming burdens of daily routine seem to melt away.

In fasting, we say "no" to some part of our experience in order to protect the deeper "yes" of our lives. This can happen in quite ordinary ways. In order to be fully attentive at an important evening meeting, we skip our usual glass of wine with dinner. Finding that a weekend spent watching televised sports dulls our sense and distracts us from family activities, we cut back on TV time in favor of richer pleasures.

All of us benefit by fasting from overwork and false guilt. We fast from fears and anxieties that would hold us back from all risk. Fasting from jealousy and envy makes us more generous friends. Our fast is less about avoiding evil or denying ourselves and more about appreciating easily forgotten goods. Fasting briefly from food reminds me of the many people who go hungry, and this awareness may motivate me to contribute something essential to fellow humans in need. In the early church, "fast days" were communal exercises; by fasting together, an entire religious community reminded itself of less fortunate persons whose fasts were less chosen and more continuous. Thus, fasting was linked to compassion and justice. The disciplines of the fast, like those of the feast, are meant to be communal exercises, not private practices.

The spiritual discipline of fasting—whether with our diets, or our work rhythms, or our intimate lives—is often a chosen practice. At times, an unhealthy false fasting intrudes into our lives. We may fall into a pattern of avoiding close relationships, and through shyness or shame, we hold ourselves aloof from contacts that might make us more fully alive. Or perhaps we descend into a depression, another unchosen fast. The cult of feminine thinness in U.S. culture manipulates young women into desperate fasts that end in eating disorders and other debilitating abuses. We find no delight or pleasure when such gruesome fasts envelope us.

Other, more painful fasts await us. A friendship is broken or a loved one dies and we are deprived of the grace of these relationships. As we mourn their loss, our fast wears the mask of grief, but even in grief we can detect the rhythms of fasting and feasting. Several years ago, a close friend died from cancer at age forty-five. Her many friends were grief stricken. Together we entered a prolonged fast, now bereft of her graceful presence. The feast that characterized a lovely friendship had ended.

Several weeks later, friends gathered again at her gravesite for the installation of the headstone. After a brief prayer, many returned to her previous home, where quiet conversation continued the mood of mourning. Months later, at the first anniversary of her death, we gathered again to recall this beloved friend whose life we had all shared. We still remembered her pain and final suffering, but at this time we were finally ready to celebrate with wine and some of her favorite foods. Now we would feast, giving thanks for the privilege of knowing and loving this remarkable woman. The fast was ended, the feast rejoined.

These rhythms, running through every life, will from time to time confound us, but as often charm us, reminding us of the mystery of our unique life journey. Navigating the shifting currents, we ride the graceful enchantment of our days.

Resources

We have visited these rhythms repeatedly in our earlier work. See, for example, our discussion of presence and absence (Chapter 13) and feasting and fasting (Chapter 15) in James and Evelyn Whitehead, *Holy Eros: Pathways to a Passionate God* (Maryknoll, NY: Orbis Books, 2009). We consider the enigma of scarcity and abundance in Chapter 3 of that book.

1. David Ford, *Self and Salvation* (Cambridge: Cambridge University Press, 1999), 113.

CHAPTER FOUR

Catholic Novelists and Their Faux Enchantments

> *If there is a reason for the existence of the novelist on earth it is this: to show the element which holds out against God in the highest and noblest characters . . . and also to light up the secret sources of sanctity in creatures which seem to us to have failed.*
>
> Francois Mauriac[1]

M ANY CATHOLIC NOVELISTS in the first half of the twentieth century found themselves apologists for God in a godforsaken world. The sacred enchantment of their faith— God's grace poured out through the church's sacraments— conflicted with the seductive enchantments of the world all around them—"the world, the flesh and the devil" of traditional Catholic piety. Evelyn Waugh described his goal in writing *Brideshead Revisited*: "to trace the divine purpose in a pagan world."[2] Walker Percy judged, "the present age is demented."[3] Their stories celebrated the healing charm of God's grace at play in a world of faux enchantments on offer in their surrounding society (faux, that is, not simply false, but counterfeit, pretending but failing to attain genuine enchantment).

Evelyn Waugh's 1944 masterpiece *Brideshead Revisited* is a fable about enchantments, human and divine. An Oxford student Charles Ryder falls in with the charming Sebastian Flyte, son of a rich, eccentric Catholic family. "I was in search of love in those days, and I went full of curiosity [hoping to] find that low door in the wall . . . which opened on an enclosed and enchanted garden."[4]

This is an adolescent romance built on skipped classes and picnics of strawberries and champagne. And it is an enchantment that cannot last. Sebastian's alcoholism and conflicts with his dysfunctional family defeat his own best hopes. Years later, looking back at the earlier idyllic time, Charles reflects, "It is thus I like to remember Sebastian, as he was that summer, when we wandered alone together through that enchanted palace."[5]

The heading of Part One announces the novel's perspective: *Et in Arcadia, Ego.* This Latin phrase ("I too was there in that idyllic place"), with death as the speaker, conveyed the message that in every enchanted garden lurk reminders of our mortality. Human attachments and human enchantments, whatever their temporary charm, cannot endure.

In Part Two of the novel, Charles Ryder enters into an adulterous affair with Sebastian's sister, Julia. This too will turn out to be a faux enchantment that cannot last. The heading of the second half of the novel, "With a Twitch of the Thread," alludes to a short story by G. K. Chesterton in which a clever detective allows a criminal to continue his misdeeds until the detective finally reels him in with the jerk of a fishing line. Waugh's novel pictures God as a kind of "hound of heaven"[6] who allows sinners a long leash before rescuing them from their sinful lives. Waugh makes this orientation clear with the stark remark: "There is only one Actor."[7]

Waugh sets this sober appraisal of the faux enchantments of human love against two symbols of the genuine enchantments provided by his Catholic faith. The first is the sacrament of the last rites (in his day, Extreme Unction). Sebastian's mother is anointed with this reconciling sacrament at her death, as is Sebastian at the point of his own death. Sebastian's father, after years of dissolute living with his mistress in Venice, returns to Brideshead to die, only after receiving the last sacraments of the church. Waugh gives great attention to the drama of the old reprobate being saved from eternal punishment by this last second sacrament.

The second symbol of a sacred enchantment is the sanctuary lamp, whose glow signals the presence of Christ in the Blessed Sacrament. Part One concludes with a somber closing of the family chapel at Brideshead after Sebastian's mother dies. Here, the final act is the extinguishing of the sanctuary lamp. And the novel ends with Charles, now a world-weary soldier, returning by chance to the area near Brideshead. Charles finds, to his great surprise, that the sanctuary lamp in the Marchmain's once-shuttered chapel has been lit again. This sacred light, extinguished countless times in history and relit once again, represents to Charles—and to Waugh—a sacred enchantment that outshines every human would-be enchantment.

More Faux Enchantments

Graham Greene, in his novel *The End of the Affair* (1952), tells a story that is suspended in a similar very Catholic tension. Maurice Bendrix enters an affair with his friend's wife, Sarah. Each has had affairs before, and such an arrangement, with no strings attached, suited them both. The terms of the affair were clear. "We had agreed so happily to eliminate God from our world."[8] But the relationship that ensued unsettled this hedged arrangement. They had agreed not to fall in love, but fall they do. They came to want more than an affair could produce, and these nonbelievers found they could not so easily evade the God who haunted their lives.

The heart of the novel is the German bombing of London and Sarah's terror that her lover, who has just left their hotel room, has been killed when a bomb hits their building. Falling on her knees, the agnostic Sarah prayed, "I'll give him up forever, only let him be alive." Bendrix has survived the explosion, and returning to the room and seeing his lover on her knees, he wonders whom she could be praying to. "To anything that might exist," [9] she responds. Startled and grateful that God has heard her prayer, Sarah determines to end the affair. But Sarah and Maurice later take up the affair once again. When Sarah becomes seriously ill she determines, yet again, to bring about the end of the affair. Before dying she receives the last sacraments.

Greene has crafted a novel that illumines how affairs fit a disenchanted world: people find moments of temporary delight in a world that offers nothing richer. But a couple may fall, accidentally, in love and begin yearning for more from each other. The enchantment of genuine love—which asks and expects everything—renders an affair deeply unsatisfying. After their affair has ended the first time, Bendrix is tempted to begin an affair with another woman to fill the empty space in his heart. But he finds, sitting beside an attractive young woman, "I felt no desire for her at all. It was as if quite suddenly after all the promiscuous years I had grown up. My passion for Sarah had killed simple lust for ever. Never again would I be able to enjoy a woman without love." [10]

Waugh's Charles Ryder and Greene's Maurice Bendrix both find frustration in romantic enchantments that cannot endure. The sacred enchantment of the sacraments offers release from these affairs. In the end, both succumb to the relentlessly pursuing God so familiar to Catholics in the first half of the century. They are failed atheists.

A Novel of Disenchantment

Another Catholic novelist at mid-century, Walker Percy, tried his hand at describing in great detail the life of a person utterly immersed in disenchantment. In *The Moviegoer* (1961), Percy paints a portrait of modern disenchantment in the metaphor of everydayness. Binx Bolling suffers from a chronic depression that is associated with his inability to find any substantial purpose in life.

Percy names two strategies of distraction that Binx employs to hold off his despair. He goes regularly to the movies (hence, the title of the novel), finding that the cinematic lives in the theater provide some brief relief from life's boredom. Movie-going functions as a faux enchantment that assuages, for the moment, the blight of his depression and despair. The other faux enchantment is his superficial flirtation with his serially hired secretaries (Marcia, Linda, Sharon). Nothing ever comes of these would-be affairs, but they do hold off for the moment the descent back into the distress of everydayness.

The novel concludes with a sudden about-face that remained unconvincing to his editor and many readers. Shriven of the need to fit in, to please others, Binx discovers that he is suddenly free. This deliverance allows Binx to commit himself to marry Kate in all her vulnerability. They are now able to emerge from the cloud of disenchantment that had haunted both of their lives.

Like Charles Ryder in *Brideshead Revisited* and Maurice Bendrix in *The End of the Affair*, Binx Bolling makes a show of rejecting religious belief; he struggles to adjust to a disenchanted life. But the effort cannot prevail. Like these other literary creations by Catholic authors in the first half of the twentieth century, Binx is a failed atheist.

These novels illustrate a Catholic spirituality that was common at mid-century. Catholics lived an insular faith, deeply suspicious of a cultural environment that seemed to threaten their beliefs. God was often presented as a severe if merciful judge, a "hound of heaven" tracking down sinful humans. In a life of faith, happiness seemed like an illusory ideal. Sebastian in *Brideshead Revisited* ponders the lives of his family members, each broken in a distinctive way, and concludes, "happiness seems to have nothing to do with it." [11]

A Seismic Shift

Even as Waugh's *Brideshead Revisited,* Greene's *The End of the Affair,* and Percy's *The Moviegoer* were enjoying much success at mid-century, a shift in Catholic spirituality was under way. Other authors, writing in the middle and second half of the century, illustrate this emerging vision of a more earthly enchantment.

Dorothy Day and Thomas Merton

In her memoir, *The Long Loneliness,* Dorothy Day writes of a happiness that was both sensual and spiritual. Unlike many authors in an earlier era who had opposed the faux enchantments of human affection to divine love, Day mused that her affection for her lover was the pathway to love of God. "I have always felt that it was life with him that brought me natural happiness, that brought me to God." She writes, "I could not see that love between man and woman was incompatible with love of God." [12]

Another theme that stands out in her memoir is her thirst for life in abundance, an abundance that all are meant to share. "I wanted life and I wanted the abundant life. I wanted it for others too . . . and I did not have the slightest idea how to find it."[13] Her flourishing would have to include others as well. This focus on a life in abundance and a full life that was to be justly shared with all signaled a social activism and more engaged spirituality just arising in Catholic life at that time.

In 1941, the twenty-seven-year-old Thomas Merton decided to forsake the world and enter the solitude of a Trappist monastery. In his best-selling memoir, *The Seven Storey Mountain* (published in 1948), Thomas Merton wrote of his longing for a community of believers "who had banded themselves together to form a small, secret colony of the Kingdom of Heaven in this earth of exile."[14]

In the years after entering the monastery, Merton's attention began to shift from a world-rejecting asceticism to a concern for the world beyond the sanctuary of his monastic life. In *Seeds of Contemplation* (published in 1949, one year after *The Seven-Storey Mountain*) we hear the first stirrings of this new interest. "I will never be able to find myself if I isolate myself from the rest of mankind as if I were a different kind of being."[15]

During the 1960s Merton gave more attention to the new enthusiasm in the church for interreligious dialogue. In the January 1961 issue of *Jubilee,* Merton wrote an article on "Classic Chinese Thought," in which he described Confucianism and Daoism as deeply ethical, religious thought and argued that Catholic colleges in the United States should have courses in these traditions (still seen by many Catholics as little more than superstition). He had now moved outside his monastery's walls, newly attuned to the enchantment of faiths well beyond the Catholic heritage.

Jacques Maritain and Pierre Teilhard de Chardin

During these middle years of the twentieth century, the French authors Jacques Maritain and Pierre Teilhard de Chardin brought to American Catholic readers a refreshing new vision of the dynamics at play in religious faith. Maritain was writing about a Christian humanism that exuded an optimistic vision of the culture that surrounded and even fed religious faith. "What the world needs is a new humanism, a 'theocentric' or integral humanism which would consider man in all his natural grandeur and weakness, in the entirety of his wounded being inhabited by God, in the full reality of nature, sin and sainthood." [16] This concept, unfamiliar to American Catholics at mid-century who still inhabited a rather insular and defensive faith, implied a certain comfort with the culture in which Catholics found themselves. If they knew anything about humanism they likely associated it with atheists who insisted that humans themselves are our sole concern. The Vatican II text on the church in the modern world, written in the early 1960s, spoke to a new openness to all humans and their deepest aspirations: "nothing that is genuinely human fails to find an echo in their [Christian] hearts." [17] Maritain's essays would help Catholics reclaim this optimism about God's presence within every culture.

To Teilhard de Chardin the entire universe was enchanted, animated by the guiding presence of God's Spirit. This dynamic presence moves the universe through an evolution that continues to gather up matter into a spiritual consciousness, pointing to a final unification of all things in Christ. In this vision, evolution is not a mindless expansion of matter but the very cosmic process where the history of salvation is being played out. And in this realization humans were discovering that they were evolution becoming conscious of itself.

Teilhard insisted that Christian life is not a matter of individual devotion or a private piety but a collaborative and collective ascent of all humanity toward a final unity in God. No evolutionary future awaits anyone except in association with everyone else. It would take some decades for this sense of cosmic enchantment to begin to find its way into the awareness of American Catholics.

Mary Gordon and Marilynne Robinson

In the latter part of the century, two Christian novelists began creating stories that spelled out this emerging conviction about a sacred enchantment deep within everyday world. *Final Payments*, Mary Gordon's 1978 novel, quite intentionally charts the shift taking place in Catholic spirituality and practice after Vatican II. Isabel Moore, Gordon's central character in the novel, lives with her widowed father, whose faith is expressed in a clear and forceful fashion: "He believed in hierarchies; he believed that truth and beauty could be achieved only by a process of chastening and exclusion." Mr. Moore believed that "One did not look for happiness on earth; there was a glory in poverty."[18] This was very much the Catholic imagination that served Waugh and Greene. Isabel, unable to embrace the certainties of her father's faith and unwilling to practice the pieties of the family's housekeeper, Margaret, struggles to find a more fitting expression of her Catholic faith.

Isabel began to see the unconscious bargain she had made in devoting her life to her infirm father: in this self-erasing sacrifice, she "had bought sanctuary by giving up youth and freedom, sex and life."[19] This decade of devotion was, in fact, a faux enchantment: what appeared to be the utmost piety became a place of hiding from life. After years of this misguided piety she hears in the Gospel story of Jesus being anointed by the woman who intrudes into a banquet a message for her own life. "I knew now I must open the jar of ointment. I must open my life." She began to recognize that the sensual might serve as portal to the sacred. "We must not deprive ourselves, our loved ones, of the luxury of our extravagant affections."[20] Extravagance joins abundance as new vocabulary in the narrative of Christian spirituality.

Like Mary Gordon, novelist Marilynne Robinson celebrates the enchantment to be found in everyday life. To do this, Robinson (a self-confessed Calvinist whom we find, in her deeply sacramental vision of reality, to be as Catholic as she is Calvinist) will focus on what she terms "rituals of the ordinary." In her first novel, *Housekeeping*, we are introduced to a widow and her children as they see to the household tasks of everyday life. The widow, still wearing the black of mourning, would carry just-washed sheets outside, hanging them up to dry in the wind and sunshine. Robinson describes such actions as "performing the rituals of the ordinary as an act of faith."[21] In the midst of such daily activity "the wind that billowed her sheets announced to her the resurrection of the ordinary." The everyday task of washing sheets—and relying on the wind and sun to dry them—prepares these sheets to once again enfold the family in comfort and sleep.

In her second novel, *Gilead*, an old minister watches a young laughing couple running from beneath a shower of water. "It was a beautiful thing to see, like something from a myth. I don't know why I thought of that now, except perhaps because it is easy to believe in such moments that water was made primarily for blessing, and only secondarily for growing vegetables or doing the wash."[22]

Natural light, like water, at times serves as occasion of enchantment. The old minister muses, "I was struck by the way the light felt that afternoon. I have paid a good deal of attention to light, but no one could begin to do it justice." It seemed to be "the kind of light that rests on your shoulders the way a cat lies on your lap." Yet later he wonders at the light of the moon: "The moon looks wonderful in this warm evening light, just as a candle flame looks beautiful in the light of morning. Light within light. It seems like a metaphor for something."[23]

Water and light are ordinary parts of the world that can shine with enchantment. Yet another instance of a reinvigorated spirituality, shared by Gordon and Robinson, is the emergence of laughter as a register of grace. Laughter had enjoyed little respect in the long tradition of Christian spirituality. Faith was seen as a sober affair; laughter, if noted at all, most often signaled derision and mocking laughter.

In her novel *The Company of Women*, Gordon has a young woman describe the healing taking place in her life as she "began noticing things in the world that made me laugh." And, with the older priest from whom she had been alienated, now "we laughed as we hadn't laughed in years. We got back what we were both afraid we had lost forever: our great pleasure in each other." Now at last, "our laughter met, our words clicked like champagne glasses."[24]

Throughout the twentieth century, Catholic novelists struggled to distinguish the genuine charm of a mortal life from the counterfeit enchantments that lie all around it. A cautionary mood in the first half of the century gave way in the second half to a more optimistic vision of the play of grace through everyday life. This shift allowed for the return of ancient Christian convictions about the partnership of the sensual and the spiritual, the graceful "rituals of the ordinary," and even the blessed charm of laughter.

Resources

We gave given much fuller attention to each of these authors in our earlier book *Enchanting the World* (New York: Crossroad, 2018).

1. Mauriac's definition of the (Christian) novel is quoted in Ralph McInerny, *Some Catholic Writers* (South Bend, IN: St. Augustine Press, 2007), 92.

2. Evelyn Waugh's judgment appears on the back jacket of the original paperback of *Brideshead Revisited*.

3. Walker Percy's judgment about "the demented age" appeared in his essay "Why Are You Catholic?," in *Signposts in a Strange Land* (New York: Farrar, Straus and Giroux, 1991), 306.

4. Waugh, *Brideshead Revisited*, 31.

5. Ibid., 79.

6. Francis Thompson's poem, first published in 1893, pictured God as a relentless pursuer of souls who finally tracks us down, saving us despite ourselves.

7. Waugh, *Brideshead Revisited*, 338

8. Graham Greene, *The End of the Affair* (New York: Penguin, 1951). 69.

9. Ibid., 95.

10. Ibid., 58.

11. Dorothy Day, *The Long Loneliness* (San Francisco: Harper and Row, 1952), 39.

12. Ibid., 134.

13. Ibid., 39.

14. Merton, *Seven Storey Mountain*, 383.

15. Merton, *Seeds of Contemplation* (New York: New Direction Books, 1962), 51.

16. Jacques Maritain, *The Range of Reason* (New York: Scribner, 1952), 165.

17. The Constitution on the Church in the Modern World (*Gaudium et Spes*), # 55, 231.

18. Mary Gordon, *Final Payments* (New York: Random House, 1978), 4.

19. Ibid., 231.

20. Ibid., 289.

21. Robinson, *Housekeeping,* 17–18.

22. Robinson, *Gilead*, 28.

23. Ibid., 51.

24. Gordon, *The Company of Women*, 356.

Part Two

Metaphors of Wonder

The vitality of life itself summons us to a more enchanted existence.

In Western cultures from ancient Greece to modern Europe and America the metaphor of Eros has served this function.

In the Asian cultures of China, Korea and Japan the vital energy of Qi plays a parallel role in cultural and spiritual enchantment.

Enchantment also arises when we are brought up short, even disoriented. Enigma and bewilderment may open doors to enchantment.

Today we are moving from a cultural mood of disenchantment into a re-enchantment with creation, a kind of second naïveté.

CHAPTER FIVE

Eros—Western Pathway to Enchantment

> *To explore again the profound interpenetration of* eros
> *and the spiritual life. This terribly fraught arena in West-*
> *ern Christendom, where the sexual meets the spiritual,*
> *urgently awaits the discovery of new paths to God.*
>
> Charles Taylor, *A Secular Age*

B ERNINI'S STATUE of *St. Teresa in Ecstasy* writhes with pleasure as the saint stretches upward to God. This statue
in the Santa Maria della Vittoria Church in Rome fuses the
erotic and the spiritual; ecstasy as enchantment. This sev-
enteenth-century enthusiasm for the embrace of eros and
spirit would be washed out of Catholic spirituality in the
next centuries, leaving both eros and enchantment subject
to suspicion. It is this loss that Catholic philosopher Charles
Taylor laments when he writes of "This terribly fraught
arena in Western Christendom, where the sexual meets the
spiritual. . . ."[1] The vitality of eros serves as a privileged
pathway to enchantment.

Eros and Agape

Catholics, ever anxious about sexuality, have nonetheless always believed in the enchantment of love. And they

71

know that this enchantment begins with God's generous affection. "God so loved the world . . ." (John 3:16). But the overthrownness of sexual love—both its exuberance and its befuddlement—has bound Christian affection with an abiding caution. The New Testament vocabulary of love spoke of friendship (*philia*) and a more profound, spiritual attachment (*agape*). The Greek word *eros* makes no appearance in the New Testament, perhaps a clue that it had no place there.

The metaphor of eros as the vital energy running through creation has traversed a long career: from its celebration in Plato to its banalization in much of the modern world—the erotic book store and the consolations of pornography—to the efforts of renewal in contemporary Christian life.

Eros entered the Western imagination through Greek mythology. In classic tales, Eros is the youngest of the deities, irresistible and fair, who subdues the hearts of both gods and humans. Earlier Greek creation stories cast Eros as more than the god of sensual love. Eros was the cosmic power that draws the universe out of chaos, bringing together the disparate elements of reality to form the human world. The original meaning of eros, then, moves well beyond the sexual.

In these early myths, eros represented a dynamic, life-giving energy with both creative and destructive potential. Eros provided the essential vitality of life, but its force could also consume and destroy. Eros was thus honored as a divine gift but equally recognized as a source of madness (*mania*). A life without eros would be cold and empty, but the untamed passion of desire could also drive a person insane.[2]

* * * *

Eros is the vital energy that courses through the world, animating every living thing. It is the force that turns the flower to the sun, the energy that stirs humans to be in touch, to reach out and link their lives in lasting ways. Eros is the raw energy that impels an infant to seize a bright marble lying in the dirt and put it into her mouth. Eros wants to touch, taste, and even consume.

* * * *

When Jewish scholars translated the Hebrew texts into Greek, they faced the question of how to translate the Bible's many stories of sensual affection and erotic love. They knew that Eros was a god, but it was not their God. Thus the word does not appear in the Hebrew Scriptures— with one exception.

In the Book of Proverbs we are introduced to a married woman "whose feet do not stay at home." She invites a man, "Come, let us take our fill of love until morning, let us delight ourselves with *eros*, for my husband is not at home" (Septuagint Greek translation of Proverbs 7:18). In its unique appearance in the Bible, eros was assigned its reputation as an adulterous passion.

The reality of eros as the vital energy that animates creation is not absent from the Bible, but this volatile force, its reputation already compromised by the many myths in the surrounding Greek culture, often appears in disguise. The Song of Songs is the most erotic book in the Bible. But even here, as biblical translators sought a vocabulary for love, they avoided the term *eros*. Instead, they selected another Greek word—*agape*—to name the lovers' sensual delight and physical affection in this sacred poem.

> His eyes are like doves by water ducts. . . . His loins are smoothest ivory. . . . His legs marble pillars. . . . His mouth is sweet and all of him is delectable. (Song of Songs 5:12, 14–16)

This poem celebrates the couple's passionate affection with no mention of children and little reference to marriage. Deeply in love, they praise one another's physical beauty and delight in each other's presence. Their relationship is profoundly mutual, and often the woman initiates the erotic exchange.

This highly erotic text confounded both Jewish and Christian scholars. Its imagery, so charged with sexual connotations, made many uncomfortable, but since its author was understood to be the great king Solomon, the religious community felt compelled to accept the text.

If the text were to be revered, special interpretation would be required. Perhaps, they suggested, the sexual imagery was an allegory for the powerful love between God and human souls. The poem could be redeemed by understanding its true focus as spiritual devotion, not the sweaty, passionate affection of two human lovers. So began the tradition of "spiritualizing" the erotic impact of this story.

If the Greek term *eros* is missing in the New Testament, the passionate engagement it describes is not absent. In various Gospel stories Jesus displays again and again a passionate care for others, especially the sick and the outsider. He is filled with the passion of regret when, near the end of his life, he looks out over Jerusalem; his anger flares in the face of hypocrisy and injustice. All these can be seen as surges of eros.

* * * *

Eros names our desire for closeness, the visceral hope that moves us out of solitude and motivates us to chance the risky relationships of friendship and love. Eros is about union—with the beautiful other, with a suffering person, with the world of nature waiting to be embraced and protected.

* * * *

As generations of Christians reflected on Jesus's compassion and generous love that the Gospels had named *agape*, they came to interpret this love as deeply spiritual—and, importantly, neither erotic nor sexual. Gradually a dualism of two kinds of love insinuated itself into the Christian heritage. The love named *agape* was seen as generous, self-giving, and spiritual. The love called *eros* was often pictured as a passionate, selfish, and sometimes sinful attraction. This dichotomy fit comfortably into other divisions taking root in Christian piety: flesh and spirit; body and soul. Growing from such dichotomies was a deep suspicion about the body's holiness, about the goodness of sex, and about the relation of spirituality and sexuality.

In the 1930s Anders Nygren published what looked like the last word on the question of Christian love. In *Agape and Eros* the Swedish Lutheran bishop opposed the self-giving affection of *agape* to the sexual and more self-centered love of *eros*. This dualism was quickly contested by critics such as Martin D'Arcy in England, but the dichotomy, so neat and seemingly inspiring, caught on and cemented Christian hesitation about erotic love.[3]

Happily, this false dualism has fallen away as Christians and others have come to a richer appreciation of the complexity of loving. If God loves with the spiritual love of *agape*—loving all humanity and playing no favorites—God also loves each person particularly and passionately, and this merits the name of eros.

Reclaiming Eros

In his first official pastoral letter, *God Is Love* (2005),[4] Pope Benedict XVI added his authority to those seeking to heal this rift between a spiritual *agape* and a sensual *eros*. More than twenty times in the letter the pope uses eros to describe both human affection and God's passionate attachments to humanity. His letter begins with a reference to eros as "that love between man and woman which is neither planned nor willed, but somehow imposes itself upon human beings" (§12). He recognizes the rich ambiguity of this force that "somehow imposes itself" beyond a sure rational control as the source of every creative and fruitful love.

Benedict acknowledges that eros, when "reduced to 'sex' becomes a commodity . . . to be bought and sold." Like any human resource, the power of eros "needs to be disciplined and purified if it is to provide not just fleeting pleasure, but a certain foretaste . . . of that beatitude for which our whole being yearns." When it is cultivated and cared for, "eros is . . . supremely ennobled" and "becomes able to attain its authentic grandeur" (§5).

Benedict is bold enough to describe God's love for humans as eros: "God loves and his love may certainly be called eros, yet it is also totally agape." The biblical prophets, he reminds us, spoke often of "God's passion for his people using boldly erotic images" (§9). Here the pope reverses a long tradition that had defined God's love as necessarily "spiritual"—that is, nonsensual, detached, and disinterested.

Well before the pope's document, theologians such as Nathan Mitchel were emphasizing *eros* as the passionate energy that links us to our creator. Mitchel recalls the old Latin Preface for Christmas and its prayer that through "knowing God visibly" in Christ, "we might be snatched up into a love of things unseen." Here the word for love was the Latin *amor*, translating the Greek *eros*. Mitchel comments: "God's *eros* awakens our own. Worship and sacraments are thus rooted in a mutual divine/human impulse that must be called erotic."[5]

* * * *

Eros is the force that quickens our hearts when we encounter suffering and moves us to help and heal. Sex, curiosity, compassion—Eros moves through our lives in delightful and bewildering ways. To live a responsible life we will have to name and even tame this mysterious force.

* * * *

Eros in the 1960s

The decade of the 1960s was, without doubt, a period of social upheaval. Every list of transforming events is likely to include the Civil Rights Act of 1964, the gradually expanding war in Vietnam, and Woodstock at the end of the decade. Some Catholics still mourn the cultural changes, especially in attitudes toward sexuality, which unsettled this decade. The feminist insurgency early in the decade (Betty Freidan's *The Feminine Mystique,* 1963) and the gay revolt at Stonewall (1969) frame the unsettling changes around sex and gender.

Joseph Bottum explains the vision of many conservative Catholics. "One understanding of the sexual revolution— the best I think—is an enormous turn against the meaningfulness of sex." For Bottum and others, "the actual effect was to disconnect sex from what previous eras had thought was the deep stuff of life: God, birth, death, heaven, hell, the moral structures of the universe, and all the rest." In his judgment, "the sexual revolution [had] brought the Enlightenment to sex, demythologizing and disenchanting the Western understanding of sexual intercourse."[6] This disenchantment meant the degrading of eros until it signaled only erotic bookstores and films.

In an earlier era the enchantment of sexuality had kept sexual expression safely encased in the guardian virtue of shame. Sexual intercourse was not only reserved for the married but for the darkened bedroom as well. It was "too sacred to talk about."[7] Taking the shame out of sex led, it seemed, to a disenchantment of sexuality itself. David Brooks comments: "One of the principal outcomes of the sexual revolution was to establish that sex is just like any other social interaction—nothing taboo or sacred about it."[8]

Abuses certainly abounded in this decade as a younger generation moved away from an inherited caution about sexuality; pornography and promiscuity flourished. But for many Catholics the decade of the 1960s was a period of exciting and positive change. Sexuality for Catholics had long been tinged with guilt and an unhealthy shame. Catholic teenagers were made aware that every "impure thought" was a mortal sin and a path to eternal punishment. Many married Catholics had learned that even their love making was necessarily marked by at least a shadow of sinfulness. It did not help that St. Augustine had famously defined marriage as "a remedy for concupiscence."

Our experience with many Catholics of our generation—those coming of age in the 1960s and 1970s—was the (re)discovery of sexuality as part of what this chapter has been calling eros—that profound, confusing, and enchanting aspect of human life. There was no disenchantment here.

In 1968, Vatican leaders called together a gathering of married Catholics and bishops to consider the question of birth control. Reversing the consensus of the study group, including the clergy among them, the Vatican then issued the encyclical *Humanae vitae*, which forbade the use of any form of artificial contraception. As an indication of the maturing conscience of lay Catholics, this decree was, then and now, largely ignored.

For some Catholics the changes taking place in the 1960s undermined a moral certitude their faith had once offered. For other Catholics a more adult embrace of sexuality returned enchantment to their sexual lives.

* * * *

Eros finds expression in our longing to close the gap between our-selves and others, our yearning to be joined to our heart's desire. Theologian James Nelson describes eros as "the yearning for fulfill-ment and deep connection . . . the divine–human energy, a drive toward union with that to which we belong."[9]

* * * *

In the spring of 2005 we were invited, while visiting in Hong Kong, to give a lecture to the Catholic clergy of the diocese. Unsure of how to proceed, we spoke of the theme of the book we were then writing: the vital energy of eros and its place in Christian spirituality. The audience was mildly engaged. Toward the end of the lecture we suggested a few tentative connections between the Western metaphor of eros and the Chinese spirituality rooted in the metaphor of the vital energy of *qi*. The room suddenly came alive; now we were talking about an enchanting force with which they were most familiar. This is the theme of the next chapter.

Resources

1. Taylor, *A Secular Age*, 767. For an earlier and fuller explora-tion of Eros, see our book *Holy Eros: Pathways to a Passionate God.*
2. Anne Carson's book *Eros the Bittersweet* (Princeton, NJ: Princeton University Press, 1986) is a hyper-literary love letter to eros. She peruses ancient Greek poetry to describe the bodily vertigo of eros ("bittersweet, limb-loosener"), and she explores

the paradox of eros: the desire for the absent other, the endless gap between oneself and the lover. Guy Davenport's essay "Eros, His Intelligence" (in *The Hunter Gracchus* [Washington, DC: Counterpoint, 1996]) is a review of Anne Carson's book. Davenport offers his definition: "Eros is the Greek for that giddy, happy, all too often frustrated conviction that another human being's returned affection and equal longing for you are all that's lacking to make life a perfect happiness" (137).

3. Anders Nygren's *Agape and Eros* (Philadelphia: Westminster Press, 1953) was first published in Sweden in the 1930s. Martin D'Arcy's *The Mind and Heart of Love* (New York: Meridian Books) appeared in 1956 after Nygren's book was published in English three years earlier.

4. Pope Benedict XVI's encyclical letter *God Is Love* (*Deus Caritas Est*) can be found at the Vatican website, www.vatican.va.

5. Nathan Mitchel, *Real Presence* (Chicago: Liturgy Training Publications, 1998), 103.

6. Bottum, "The Things We Share."

7. During the fall semesters in 2005 and 2006 we offered a series of lectures for thirty-eight Protestant ministers at Fudan University in Shanghai. The ministers were enthusiastically engaged in the group discussions of contemporary marriage and the cultural forces arrayed against it in modern China. Yet when we offered to guide a group reflection on sexuality the group demurred. When we questioned their resistance to exploring this volatile topic, their final answer was "sexuality is too sacred to talk about."

8. See David Brooks's column "The Power of Human Touch," *New York Times*, January 19, 2018, A25. Brooks is quoting an article by Elizabeth Breunig in the *Washington Post*.

9. Theologian James Nelson has written widely and well on a wide range of themes related to eros and Christian life. See especially his essay "Love, Power, and Justice in Ethics," in *Christian Ethics* (New York: Pilgrim Press, 1996), 288.

CHAPTER SIX

Qi (气)—Eastern Pathway to Enchantment

Qi is "a mysterious, vital substance/energy which binds the individual to the ultimate source of being."
Sinologist Benjamin Schwartz

IN THE CHINESE TRANSLATION of the Bible two cultural images—the vital spirit of *qi* (气) and the *dao* (道) as transcendent way—rhyme wonderfully with the metaphors at the heart of Christian faith. Qi names the mysterious energy that animates all creation; it is the life force that the creator breathes into Adam. *Dao* names the way, likewise mysterious yet available to anyone paying attention to the path of their life; in the Chinese rendering of John's Gospel we read, "in the beginning was the Dao" (1:1).[1]

Through the heart of the Chinese worldview runs a vital energy that is named with the single sound *qi* or *ch'i* (气).[2] Many Westerners are familiar with *feng shui* (literally, wind/water), the distinctive Chinese concern to situate buildings, from homes to bank buildings, in their proper relation to the force of the passing wind and water. This is a question of harmonizing the environment with the spiritual energy of *qi*. Chinese everywhere delight in performing the graceful exercises of *tai ji chuan*; this too is a matter of attuning oneself to the vital flow of *qi* through the body. Traditional Chinese medicine, from acupuncture to *qi gong,* trains its attention on the healthy flow of bodily energy that is *qi.* China scholar Benjamin Schwartz, after offering the definition in the epigram above, adds, "ch'i in itself is discussed in the rapturous language of the mystic."[3] This is a force as enchanting as it is mysterious.

A clue to the elusive meaning of this energy lies in the traditional Chinese character itself. It pictures a steaming kettle that contains a kernel of rice (氣). At the top of the character we see the heat of the fire causing the kettle's lid to flap, remembering that rice is not edible until boiled. And we recall that the energy of heat leads both to nourishment and potential scalding. Not incidentally, one of the Chinese terms for anger is *sheng qi*—"energy rising." Or, we might say, "getting steamed."

In the first pages of this chapter we will revisit two ancient authors and their view of *qi.* Zhuangzi, a founding father of Daoism, and Mencius, the first great Confucian philosopher, both lived during the fourth century BCE. Their ideas continue today to fascinate readers in both the East and the West.

We will then consider how Christians, both Chinese and Western, have attempted to harmonize this distinctively Chinese notion of vital energy with biblical passages that speak of God's creative, healing power as breath, wind, and Spirit. Finally, we reflect on the resonance between the Western metaphor of eros and the Chinese image of *qi,* each attempting to name energies that are at once intimate, beyond measure, and enchanting.

Zhuangzi on Qi

Zhuangzi was an intellectual maverick, a contrarian, and a provocateur. He was a master of bewilderment and paradox.[4] But in the midst of his mind games he provided tantalizing suggestions about the mysterious power called *qi*. In the first chapter of the book named for him, *Zhuangzi, qi* appears as a kind of cosmic wind that blows through the world, supporting the flight of transcendent figures who rise above all earthly concerns that limit humans. "Master Lieh could ride upon the wind wherever he pleased." This was because he could rely on the wind—the invisible but supportive updrafts sustaining him. This same energy also generates and dissolves the clouds that create the planet's climate. This cosmological vision of an uplifting, world-embracing energy resonates with the modern word for weather (*tian qi* in Chinese, or "heaven's energy") as a force that is essential to life, yet invisible and beyond human control. This is a typical Chinese reference to the enchanting transcendence abiding within the cosmos.

In the second chapter, Zhuangzi returns to the metaphor of *qi* as wind: "The universe has a cosmic breath (*qi*). Its name is wind." This wind blows through the hollows of trees, creating a music that is sometimes mild and other times howling. "The earth's music is the sound of these hollows." Students of ancient Greek history might remember discussions of the cosmic music provided by "the harmony of the spheres," and those familiar with St. John's Gospel may hear echoes of the description of God's Spirit "that blows where it will" (John 3:8).

In Chapter Four Zhuangzi locates this energy within humans as their animating life force. In a parable that demonstrates his typical style, a character tells his follower that in order to become wise a person must learn to fast. The follower responds, "My family is poor, and it's been several months since I've drunk wine or tasted meat. May this be considered as fasting?" But the master has another kind of fasting in mind—"a fasting of the heart" (*zhai xin*). This discipline depends on a careful listening and a gradual shedding of external distractions. "To fast with the heart one must listen not only with one's ears, but with one's heart." But a person must do yet more. "One must pay close attention not only with one's heart, but with one's vital energy (*qi*). Ears can only hear; the heart can only perceive; but a person's *qi* is empty, receptive to all things. The Dao abides in emptiness. Self-emptying is the fasting of the heart." Zhuangzi is suggesting that beneath all the worries and self-deceptions that rattle about in our hearts there resides a hollow space in which, emptied of all distraction and self-absorption, we become still, anxiety free, and newly attentive to the world around us.[5]

For Zhuangzi, the cosmic energy that creates the climate and the physiological/spiritual energy that enlivens human lives are the same force. This culture happily lacks the dualism of physical and spiritual. If a Westerner inquires, "Is *qi* physiological or spiritual?" the answer is most likely to be "yes."

Mencius on Qi

As a Confucian philosopher, Mencius was most attentive to human development. We read that his own efforts in this regard had led to his possessing, by age forty, "an unperturbed mind." This observation perplexed his listeners as it does most readers today. What does this mean? Mencius responds that he is no longer thrown off or disturbed by external fears or anxieties.[6]

China scholar Lee Yearley explores how the cosmic energy of *qi* also becomes the force that makes the virtue of courage possible. He begins by distinguishing various forms of this vital energy. *Qi*, he reminds us, was often pictured as "a circulating fluid." But, in Mencius's vision of virtue, *qi* has other dimensions: it "has potentially numinous qualities; it can be a spiritual energy when it operates in perfected human beings." In Yearley's understanding, the special flood-like *qi* "produces powerful effects, such as assurance about one's goals, added energy to reach them, and even joyful reactions while acting."[7]

Curiously, this discussion of the moral energy of *qi* then segues into a seemingly unrelated story—the famous parable of the farmer in the province of Song who foolishly ruins his own crop. This farmer has been examining his slowly developing grain day after day and, impatient with its development, finally begins to gently pull on the stalks, hoping to "help it to grow."[8] Such impatience, of course, ruins the crop. Chinese parables are never far from concerns about nourishment, and it is this notion that connects the two discussions. Mencius has been careful to nourish his moral energy of *qi*, and so it slowly develops; the farmer from Song is not so careful and his crop with all its potential nourishment is wasted.

Mencius will return to this linking of moral development with the metaphor of nourishment. In Book Six of *Mencius*, he begins with a description of the trees of a famous mountain that were once full and flourishing, having been nourished by the wind and rain. But loggers and, later, grazing cattle managed over time to devastate these beautiful trees. So it is, Mencius suggests, with human development. An unhealthy environment that consistently wears down our efforts at virtuous living leads, over time, to a deterioration of the human spirit and its sense of right and wrong.

It is here that Mencius turns to his loveliest image of the healing energy of *qi*. Even when one's moral environment has been compromised by daily distractions and unhealthy behavior, there are still certain times when a quiet epiphany may take place that reminds persons of their own best ideals. Sometimes, he writes, "in the calm air (*qi*) of the morning, just between night and day," one might gain a glimpse of "the desires and aversions that are proper to humans." But, he continues, soon the day fully dawns and concerns again distract and defeat one's sense of morality. Like the felled trees earlier in the parable, a person's moral sense may be gradually whittled away.

Of special interest to the theme of enchantment are the two appearances of the term *qi* in this parable. The moment of insight at the day's first light is described as "the *qi* of dawn." The dawn, with its refreshing air and first glimmer of light, lifts our hearts and offers reminders of who we might be. But this is a fragile vision and easily squandered as noisy events of the day accumulate and undermine resolve. The second appearance of *qi* suggests a complementary role for this *dawning* energy. The night itself contains a restorative energy; this is "the *qi* of the night." But it too can be squandered as we toss and turn, working the regrets from the day before and anxieties about the day to come.

Though we may be buffeted by worries and anxieties day and night, morality-bracing *qi* arrives both in the restoration of the night and fragile reminders glimpsed at dawn's first light. If these essential elements of morality are most often lost to the distractions and temptations of the day, they nonetheless remain available to us on a daily basis. This is the core of Mencian enchantment and spirituality.[9]

Chinese Qi and Christian Spirit

The first Christians in China puzzled over the challenge of translating Christian belief into Chinese idioms. The

Hebrew of the Old Testament and the Greek of the New Testament belonged to radically different thought worlds than the Chinese language.

Problems began at the very beginning of Scripture. In the Book of Genesis God is pictured as creating the first human by breathing into the clay shaped like a human form (Genesis 2;7). With this animating breath, the clay (*adamah* in Hebrew) became a living human being. Chinese translators of the Bible saw that the divine breath (*ruah* in Hebrew) was not unlike the cosmic, world-animating energy of *qi* in their own culture. Each was a mysterious power that transcended humans. Thus we read in some Chinese translations of this passage: God breathed into Adam's nostrils "lifegiving *qi*" (*sheng qi*). Until this biblical translation, *qi* had been a uniquely Chinese concept, hermetically contained within this culture's vision of reality. With this translation, the enchanting Chinese metaphor found its way into the mouth of God. It now belonged to Christian belief as much as to Chinese culture.

Nor was this usage a one-time event. In the Book of Exodus God's power in rescuing the Israelites from Egypt was described, in Hebrew, in the imagery of breath: "A blast from your nostrils and the waters piled high. You blew with your breath (*qi*), and the sea closed over them" (Exodus 15:8, 10). Just as the vital energy of *qi* in Zhuangzi creates weather that nourishes and at times destroys, so the breath of God creates but is capable of destroying.

Near the end of the Gospels we meet two instances of breath as *qi*. On the cross Jesus breathes his last. "Father, into your hands I commend my spirit, and bowing his head he breathed out his last breath (*duan qi*)" (Luke 23:46). In St. John's Gospel the risen Jesus gathers his disciples and, after instructing them, "breathes upon them" (*yi kou qi*; one mouthful of *qi*) (John 20:22). This dramatic gesture intentionally echoes the breath of life in the Book of Genesis that marked the first gasp of human life.

The image of a divine, creative breath is elsewhere in Scripture joined by the image of God's Spirit moving through the world with mysterious force. Zhuangzi, as we saw, had described such a cosmic wind, both powerful and invisible, moving through the world. John's Gospel turns to a similar image: the Spirit of God moving through the world like a breeze: "the wind blows where it chooses. You can hear the sound of it, but you do not know where it comes from or where it goes" (John 3:8). In both texts, we are introduced to a mysterious force that both transcends and enchants humans.

Chinese Theologians Today

Aloysius Chang, a Catholic theologian in Taiwan, observes how the Chinese cultural image of *qi* meets Christian belief: "*ch'i* or spirit belongs not only to the cosmic and natural life-world, but it is also closely connected with the moral dimension of human life . . . it serves as the mysterious bridge between God and the human person."[10]

Hong Kong theologian Madeleine Kwong Lai Kuen has written an extraordinary reflection on a theology of the Holy Spirit in "a way that better conforms to Chinese wisdom." Displaying a deep knowledge of Christian theology as well as a rich appreciation of her own culture's values, Professor Kwong presents a careful investigation of "the notion of *qi* [that] is close to the biblical concept of [Hebrew] *ruah*, [Greek] *pneuma*, the breath of God."[11]

Kwong defines *qi* as "a force that is all-present and all-penetrating, animating and stimulating, creative and transformative, both powerful and gentle, expressible and ineffable, a dynamic that is at once cosmic and human, inter-

nal and external." Kwong revisits the richness and range of
qi throughout the long tradition of Chinese thought. Not
only does the notion of *qi* represent an omnipresent and
transforming power within reality—embracing cosmological, physiological, medical, ethical, and aesthetic domains—
but *qi* names a mysterious force that is more than a concept
or category of thought; that is, in fact, "a lived reality, a vital
experience in everyday life." An advantage of *qi*, apart from
its widespread acceptance by Chinese of every historical
period and intellectual persuasion, is that this notion has
never borne explicitly religious connotations; its provenance
is more cultural than explicitly religious.

Throughout this work Kwong is presenting an inculturation of Christian belief within the Chinese culture. She
suggests that the Holy Spirit is the presence of God that,
being least personal and least masculine, is most open to the
Chinese culture's convictions about the mysterious, animating force that Christians name God. Unlike its trinitarian
partners, Father and Son, the Holy Spirit has always been
pictured in traditional, orthodox theology as an animating,
nongendered force active throughout creation. The biblical
metaphors of the Holy Spirit—especially breath and wind—
bring it close to Chinese convictions about the pervasive
power of *qi*.

Kwong's sophisticated approach acknowledges that the
resonance between Christian theology's portraits of the
Spirit and the Chinese culture's imagery of *qi* is just that:
a cross-cultural resonance, not an identification. "Obvi-
ously, we do not mean to say that the Chinese *qi* is the Holy
Spirit. The connotation of the Chinese *qi* is never identified
with the contents of the revelation of the Spirit of God in
our Christian faith." Yet *qi*, with its "lively and evocative
image at once concrete, sensible, important and mysterious
. . . permits it to intervene into our theological research and

our attempt at inculturation." She suggests that such efforts at inculturation are important because "we Chinese Christians believe that by experiencing *qi*, we can taste subtly, and enjoy a bit more, the manifestation of the Spirit in salvation history, savor the mystery of the Spirit in the human being, and the human being in the Spirit."

China scholar Benoit Vermander offers one more helpful perspective on this enchanting vital energy: "The *qi* can somehow be defined as the power which makes everything grow according to its own nature. It is neither a 'material' nor a 'spiritual' concept. It rather points out the integrating factor behind the various spheres of natural and human development." He concludes, "the rich literature around the *qi* concept could enable Christians to internalize what the Scriptures tell them about the Spirit, its tireless circulation, its unifying function."[12]

Resources

1. The Chinese term *Dao* means both "way" and "word." This ambiguity allows for a translation of Christ as both the Word (*Logos* in the Greek of the New Testament, John 1:1) and the Way (John 14:6).

2. In Taiwan this vital energy is transliterated as *ch'i* and expressed in the traditional character 氣 . In the mainland it is rendered as *qi* and expressed in the simplified pinyin form 气 . The pronunciation in Mandarin Chinese is the same.

3. Benjamin Schwartz's remark at the beginning of the chapter appears in his *The World of Thought in Ancient China* (Cambridge, MA: Harvard University Press, 1985), 270. His further definition appears in his *China and Other Matters* (Cambridge, MA: Harvard University Press, 1996), 80.

4. A favorite gambit for Zhuangzi (this is the spelling of his name in the mainland; elsewhere Chuang Tzu is the spelling) is the taunting question: "what is the use of the useless?" He tells fables of old, twisted trees that are "good for nothing," and so have been neglected by loggers and carpenters to live out a long

life (Chapters One and Four). And he recalls the disabled man who, being useless for the military, finds his disability ensuring him a long life (Chapter Four). Zhuangzi concludes, "Such is the usefulness of the useless." See Book Four, p. 35 of *The Book of Chuang Tzu*, trans. Martin Palmer (New York: Penguin, 2006).

5. *The Book of Chuang Tzu*, Book One, p. 3; Book Two, p. 8; Book Four, p. 29.

6. *Mencius*, 2A2, 33, trans. D. C. Lau (New York: Penguin, 2003).

7. Lee Yearley, *Mencius and Aquinas: Theories of Virtue and Conceptions of Courage* (Albany, NY: State University of New York Press, 1990), 152.

8. *Mencius*, 2A2, 33.

9. *Mencius*, 6A8, 127.

10. Chang is quoted by Hans Küng and Julia Ching in their *Christianity and Chinese Religion* (New York: Doubleday, 1989), 266. For fuller explorations of Chang's thought on this mysterious power, see "Ch'i and Some Theological Themes," in *Collectanea Theologica Universitatis Fujen* 53 (1982): 341–68.

11. Kwong Lai Kuen, *Qi chinois et anthropologie chrétienne* (Paris: L'Harmattan, 2000), 187. Other quotations from her work appear on pages 10 and 11.

12. Benoit Vermander, "Theologizing in the Chinese Context," in *Studia Misssionalia* 45 (1996): 128.

CHAPTER SEVEN

Back Channels to Enchantment

Enigma does not block understanding but provokes it.[1]

"FOR NOW WE SEE in a mirror, darkly [*enigma*], but then we will see face to face. Now I know in part, but then I will know fully" (1 Corinthians 13:12). Saint Paul resorts to the Greek word *enigma* to point to the puzzlement that haunts our *seeing darkly*. He is predicting that we can catch a glimpse of deeper truths, though our perception may be slightly distorted (as in a mirror) and often muddled (as in a cloudy mirror). Is this *darkly knowing* a deficit in our mind's design or an alert that we are approaching a reality that defies our comprehension?

If enchantment often elicits a romantic resonance, there are less comforting experiences—enigma, bewilderment, and elegy—that open doors to enchantment. Literary critic George Steiner links enigma with enchantment when he writes of "the enigma of creation as it is made sensible in the poem, in the painting, in the musical statement."[2] Philosopher Roberto Unger describes "the enigma of our existence" that is rooted in the endless tension between longing and jeopardy. We are drawn with longing toward every kind of association with others, aware of the jeopardy of such endeavors: the danger of being absorbed or manipulated or disappointed.[3]

Saint Paul reminds us that enigma is an unavoidable aspect of our relationship with God whose "ways are inscrutable" (Romans 11:33). The wisdom literature in the Hebrew Scripture is designed to remind us that life itself is a puzzlement we will never fully unravel. But there is some consolation to be found in this *darkly knowing*. "The knowledge [spiritual insight] gives is not like a noonday sun but . . . like the light of a candle in a dark room, sufficient to see our way—to make the moral commitment of faith that we are called to exercise as persons in a moral universe." [4]

In the Hebrew Bible, one man raised new and disturbing questions about the enigma of suffering. The story of Job tells us about a wealthy and pious man with a large family and many possessions. Suddenly, he is struck by significant troubles: crop failure, the death of family members, extensive personal ailments. As his suffering accumulates, Job struggles to understand this sudden change of events. What has he done to deserve this?

In the conventional wisdom of his day, suffering meant punishment for wrongdoing. Paul Ricoeur sums up this broad conviction in the ancient world: "If you suffer, if you are ill, if you fail, if you die, it is because you have sinned." [5] Any human disorder—whether physical or mental—and any disruption in nature—such as a drought or flood—brought an indictment that humans had done something wrong.

Unable to explain his torments, Job curses the day he was born. Well-meaning friends offer consolation and urge him to acknowledge his own evil deeds as the cause of his suffering. Job's children come under the same judgment: "Your children must have been evil: God has punished them for their crimes" (Job 8:4). Again, the conventional wisdom about a moral universe prevails here: suffering can arise only from sin.

Refusing to accept this account, Job turned to God in bitter lament, demanding to know the cause of his suffering. But an enigmatic God refused to offer Job an explanation for his distress. Instead, God appeared dramatically—"out of a whirlwind"—to challenge Job's audacity: "Where were you when I planned the earth? . . . Have you ever commanded morning or guided dawn to its place?" (Job 38:4, 12). Job learns that God is not answerable to his or anyone else's moral code. He was reduced to silence. "I have dealt with great things I do not understand; things too wonderful for me, which I cannot know . . . therefore I disown what I have said and repent in dust and ashes" (Job 42:3). This story is meant to disorient us: this is not the God we thought we knew, about whom we had learned in religion class.

An epilogue ends the book (Job 42:7–17), offering a more uplifting conclusion to Job's confusion. The poetry of this final chapter shifts to prose, and we learn that Job's suffering was only a trial from God. Job in his patience has passed the test and is rewarded with a long life, many children and abundant sheep. We read these final paragraphs with a sigh of relief. This conclusion has the charm of a fairy tale where everything comes out fine in the end. But the epilogue would seem to undo the more mysterious theme at the heart of this biblical text. The Book of Job offers two kinds of enchantment: the consolations of a life with trials and a happy ending, and the more mysterious belonging to an utterly enigmatic God.

Bewilderment as Pathway to Enchantment

The Israelites, who escaped from slavery in Egypt, floundered in the wilderness. Lost in a land without roads they wondered where to turn. And they began to complain: how was this better than slavery, which provided meals and a place to sleep? This wilderness would, of course, become the route to a land flowing with milk and honey, but these wanderers had not yet heard that part of the story.

The Gospel of Mark, the earliest account of Jesus's life, inserts a wilderness at the very beginning. Jesus, about to begin his ministry, is led out into a wilderness where he is confronted with three different temptations (Mark 1:12–13). What could Jesus, the son of God, have to do with wilderness? In both the Hebrew Scriptures and Mark's Gospel, the wilderness is somehow connected with a refining revelation.

Wilderness comes indoors in the distressing emotion of bewilderment. The *Oxford English Dictionary* defines bewilderment as "confusion arising from losing one's way; mental confusion from inability to grasp or see one's way through a maze or tangle of impressions or ideas. . . ." Bewilderment, as an experience of disorientation, may serve as a prod to find new paths through the thicket of our lives. As a virtue, bewilderment "corrects the inclination to unwarranted certainty."[6] It is a portal to humility.

Kathryn Schulz comments, "Certainty is lethal to two of our most redeeming and human qualities: imagination and empathy." A certainty about the rightness of our ways makes any shift in perspective all but impossible. "If imagination is what enables us to conceive of and enjoy stories other than our own, and if empathy is the act of taking other people's stories seriously, certainty deadens or destroys both qualities. When we are caught up in our own convictions, other people' stories—which is to say, other people—cease to matter to us."[7] As we cling to our carefully assembled certitude, doubt becomes a luxury we feel we cannot afford. It may take a wilderness, with its diet of disorientation, to compel us to surrender our certainty and the sense of righteousness that so often rides shotgun to our confidence.

Theologian Margaret Farley writes of the "grace of self-doubt" as "one of the least recognized gifts of the Spirit." There are, of course, different kinds of self-doubt. Doubt "is a debility that can distract us, undermine our capacity for discernment, and cut the nerve of our action." There also is a graced self-doubt, however, necessary perhaps especially for those who are in positions of power. "If the greatest temptation of religious persons is self-righteousness, the second greatest is the grasping for certitude—fighting self-doubt in ways that shut the mind and sometimes close the heart." Farley observes that a virtuous self-doubt "allows us to listen to the experience of others, take seriously reasons that are alternative to our own, rethink our own last word."[8]

Christian Wiman, exploring his own search for a religious faith, writes, "Honest doubt, what I would call devotional doubt, is marked, it seems to me, by three qualities: humility, which makes one's attitude impossible to celebrate; insufficiency, which makes it impossible to rest; and mystery, which continues to tug you upward—or at least outward—even in your lowest moments. Such doubt is painful, but its pain is active rather than passive, purifying rather than stultifying."[9] Spiritual wilderness and the virtue of bewilderment are honorable elements in a mature Christian faith.

The Art of Elegy

Enigma and bewilderment instruct us in the ways of enchantment. Yet another teacher is elegy as the song of our mortality. Norman Maclean's family memoir, *A River Runs through It,* begins with the sentence, "In our family, there was no clear line between religion and fly fishing." For Maclean, both religion and fly fishing include rituals of close attention to what lies beneath; each consists of practices, whether in church or on the river, of honoring inscrutable rhythms that course through every life.

Maclean's father, a Presbyterian minister, teaches his sons to reverence the Blackfoot River that runs through the rural Montana of their family property. "The river was cut by the world's great flood and runs through rocks from the basement of time." The "it" that the river runs through is both the property where they fly fish and the larger world stretching out before and after their mortal lives. In this memoir Maclean is attempting to honor and grieve the life of his brother Paul, whose very character seemed to lead to the brutal death that cut his life short.

Novelist Annie Proulx, in her Foreword to the twenty-fifth anniversary edition of Maclean's book, catches the elegiac tone of this extraordinary piece of literature. "It is one of the rare truly great stories in American literature—allegory, requiem, memoir—and so powerful and enormous in symbol and regret for a lost time and a lost brother, for human mortality and the consciousness of beauty that it becomes part of the life experience of the reader, unforgettable." She adds, "almost no other author's work reads aloud as well as Maclean's, elegiac and haunting and taut."[10]

The link between elegy and enchantment stands out in two award-winning films from the 1980s. In the 1986 film *The Mission*, European Jesuits embark on a mission to the Guarani people of South America. The Jesuit played by Jeremy Irons sits near one of their villages and plays a haunting melody on his oboe; the music charms the natives out of their fearful resistance to these foreigners. Extraordinary natural scenery—steep cliffs to climb to reach the natives' home, precipitous water falls, a raging river—and a sense of nostalgia complement this music to generate a compelling sense of enchantment.

The Jesuits and their music enjoy some success in educating the natives and acquainting them with Christian faith, but international politics prove fatal to the Jesuits' efforts. The film's enchantment arises in its elegy for what might have been.

In the 1985 movie *Out of Africa*, we hear the voice of a Danish woman (Meryl Streep playing Karen Blixen) intoning, "I had a farm in Africa." This haunting phrase—a kind of mantra or incantation—is repeated throughout the movie. The woman's adventure in this foreign land entails a double enchantment: with an exotic land—portrayed in the repeated scenes of the extraordinary landscape of Africa and with an Englishman ("Dennis," played by Robert Redford) who makes his home in this place. As in *The Mission*, we are alerted to the fact that these enchantments cannot endure. A fire destroys the tobacco crop that Blixen has planted on her farm. Her lover dies in a plane crash. At his funeral Blixen ends her elegy with the words that describe her enchantment with Africa as well as her affair with Dennis: "he was not ours; he was not mine."

In both films, powerful music combines with extraordinary natural scenery of a foreign land and a haunting sense of nostalgia for dreams denied in order to forge a mood of enchantment. The lesson of these movies is that all human enchantments are mortal. Not necessarily faux, but mortal. And so ensues elegy and requiem.

Maclean's memoir ends with the sentence, "I am haunted by waters." This is not the haunting of ghosts or ghouls; nor is it about nightmares. Here haunting is the peculiar kind of presence that honors the enigmatic and often bewildering nature of human lives. Haunting is a metaphor for the kind of presence that expands our world as it brings the seemingly absent to our attention. Erase haunting and you are left with a disenchanted world.

Conclusion

In the deliberations at the Second Vatican Council in the 1960s, church leaders began a return to an admirable humility in the face of the enigmatic and bewildering world in which we find ourselves. Church documents spoke of the "haunting" aspect of the mysterious presence of God in the world and of "a certain awareness of a hidden power, which lies behind the course of nature and the events of human life."[11] In a text focused on the church itself, the council urged Christians to be mindful of all those "who in shadows and images seek the unknown God."[12]

Enigma, bewilderment, and elegy all abide under the mantel of the mystery that is God. Theologian John Mahoney reminds us that "it is the mystery of God which earths all theology and at the same time makes theological pluralism unavoidable." This means that theological reflection is "always and inevitably imperfect, a peering through a dark glass of human limited intelligence and limited language, such that no one glimpse or expression can encompass or exhaust the divine reality. . . ." Mahoney insists that "such a bid to recover the mystery of moral theology . . . does not leave man in agnosticism or in impenetrable darkness about moral behaviour." But what it does do "is to admonish man to a due humility in his conclusions and in his claims for himself and upon others, and to inject a note of reverence for God and the work of His hands into all moral enterprise."[13]

Historian Peter Brown recalls a significant point in early church history when this respect for mystery began to give way to an unwarranted certainty. As church leaders gathered in the early years of the fifth century to condemn Pelagius for his understanding of free will, "matters that had previously been regarded as impenetrable and as open to disagreement among experts—such as the relation between grace and free will, the exact nature of original sin, and the exact meaning of the baptism of children—were handled with peremptory certitude by Augustine and his colleagues."[14] Such unwarranted certitude would make enigma and bewilderment seem unworthy elements in Christian belief.

The re-enchantment of the world names the return, in the Catholic Church and beyond, to a humble embrace of the enigmatic and often bewildering reality around us. This return allows Christian requiems to regain a richer tone of elegy as the song of our mortal lives.

Resources

1. Paul Ricoeur, *Freud and Philosophy* (New Haven, CT: Yale University Press, 1970), 18.

2. Steiner, *Real Presences*, 4.

3. Unger, *Passion*, 123; also see 20 and 95.

4. Paul Avis, *God and the Creative Imagination* (London: Routledge, 1999), 12.

5. Paul Ricoeur, *The Symbolism of Evil* (Boston: Beacon Press, 1963), 31.

6. See Lee Yearley's essay on "Ethics of Bewilderment" in the *Journal of Religious Ethics* 38 (2019): 441.

7. Kathryn Schulz, *Being Wrong: Adventures in the Margin of Error* (New York: HarperCollins, 2010), 164, 167.

8. Margaret Farley, "Ethics, Ecclesiology, and the Grace of Self-Doubt," in *A Call to Fidelity* (Washington, DC: Georgetown University Press, 2002), 68–69.

9. Christian Wiman, *My Bright Abyss: Meditation of a Modern Believer* (New York: Farrar, Straus and Giroux, 2013), 76.

10. See the twenty-fifth anniversary edition of Norman Nackean's *A River Runs through It* (Chicago: University of Chicago Press, 2001). The quotations from the memoir are on pp. 1 and 104. Proulx's observations are on p. xi of the Foreword.

11. "Declaration on the Relation of the Church to Non-Christian Religions " (*Nostra aetate*), *Documents of Vatican II*, 570.

12. Constitution on the Church (*Lumen gentium*), §16, *Documents of Vatican II*, 22.

13. John Mahoney, *The Making of Moral Theology* (Oxford: Clarendon Press, 1987), 340.

14. Peter Brown, *Through the Eye of a Needle: Wealth, the Fall of Rome, and the Making of Christianity in the West, 350–550 AD* (Princeton, NJ: Princeton University Press, 2012), 369.

CHAPTER EIGHT

The Re-enchantment of the World

Beyond the desert of criticism, we wish to be called again.[1]

THE CHRISTIAN INHABITANTS of western Europe in the year 1500 lived in an enchanted world—a "world of spirits, demons, and moral forces."[2] Spirits inhabited mountains and streams. An earthquake or flood could be "read" as a moral judgment of its victims. A child born blind might be seen as representing the sin of its parents. Ingmar Bergman's film *The Virgin Spring* (1960), set in fourteenth-century Sweden, captured this lived reality. A young woman, while walking through a forest, is attacked, raped, and murdered. Soon in the very clearing where she had been killed a natural spring began to bubble up from the ground. In an enchanted world, nature itself weeps for the violence committed there while cleansing the site with pure water. Nature's movements resonate with moral judgments.

This enchanted world began to fray in the face of Galileo's scientific analysis of heavenly bodies. People were invited to reckon with their planet as not occupying the center of the universe. The inherited and enchanted world with heaven above and hell below came under review. Later, Darwin's theory of evolution contradicted long-cherished Christian beliefs both about the age of the world and humanity's privileged place at its origin. Perhaps we humans are not the pinnacle of creation, but creatures risen from a long line of mammals.

The emergence of modern science transformed our world in profound ways, from improvements in bodily health to knowledge of the solar system. But a corollary of this positive development was a disenchantment with an earlier human worldview. As science developed, Christians were challenged to find God in a radically altered worldview. One strategy was to separate the natural world from the supernatural realm. *Nature*—the visible, measurable reality around us—came to be seen as a self-sustaining reality that was governed by its own laws; this arena could be safely ceded to science. *Grace*—what we confess today as the surprising gift of God's presence—was then pictured as a scarce and miraculous substance that God imparted to the world. Faith, quite apart from reason, existed in the reserved zone of the supernatural, safe from the invasive inquiries of scientists and rationalists. Gone was the sixteenth-century Christian humanism so optimistically on display in Ignatius Loyola's conviction about "finding God in all things," and the fusion of the sensual and the spiritual in the Bernini's statue of *St. Teresa in Ecstasy*.

This dualism of nature and grace, meant to defend God's own sovereignty in a rapidly changing climate, came at a high price. Louis Dupré describes the consequences of this split: theologians, "concerned that a too intimate connection with the material world would compromise God's absolute transcendence, removed God from the natural world" and "the divine became relegated to a sphere separate from nature."[3]

Paul Ricoeur has described this long season of cultural and religious disenchantment as "a desert of criticism."[4] Deprived of their enchanted world, many Christians found it difficult to sustain their faith in the midst of this new cultural climate. Invoking the biblical imagery of the desert, Ricoeur reminds Jews and Christians that in their heritage this arid expanse is neither a cul-de-sac nor a final destination, but a way station to renewed life. As early as the Book of Deuteronomy the people of Israel were reminded of their past deserts, both harrowing and hopeful. "[God] made water flow for you from flint rock and fed you in the wilderness with manna that your ancestors did not know, to humble you and test you, and in the end to do you good" (Deuteronomy 8:15–16).

For many people today this desert of criticism endures, with its sense that the world is only what we see and nothing more. Yet for many others, there remains an awareness, often tentative and unclear, that reality includes *more than meets the eye*. Many today are recovering a sense of the mystery imbedded in the world around us. Paradoxically, it is the very advance of science that is opening the door to a humbler and more tentative way of believing.

Re-enchanting the World

In 1963, three years after Bergman's film *The Virgin Spring*, Rachel Carson published *Silent Spring*, her exposé of the toxic effect of pesticides. Readers were astonished to learn these potent chemicals not only killed the targeted pests but continued their destruction of the environment, leeching into streams and destroying fish and other organisms. "We poison the gnats in a lake and the poison travels from link to link of the food chain and soon the birds of the lake margin become its victims."[5] Her research on soil—the life-filled loam so essential for agriculture of all kinds—distinguished it from lifeless dirt. Now the earth itself began to seem enchanted. Seven years prior to her award-winning *Silent Spring,* Carson had published a book that was closer to her profession as a marine biologist. In *The Edge of the Sea* Carson reflected on the marginal world where the sea meets the shore—what she called "that enchanted place on the threshold of the sea." Her study of the many creatures who inhabit this zone made her aware that in "the beauty of the spectacle there has meaning and significance. It is the elusiveness of the meaning that haunts us, that sends us again and again into the natural world where the key to the riddle is hidden." In the final paragraphs of this book she returns to her sense of wonder. "Contemplating the teeming life of the shore, we have an uneasy sense of the communication of some universal truth that lies just outside our grasp." And the scientist ends the book with this observation: "The meaning haunts and ever eludes us, and in its very pursuit we approach the ultimate mystery of Life itself."[6] Historian Jill Lepore notes the rare combination of scientific precision and literary style in Carson's books. Careful analysis joined a poetic enchantment that made the book an instant success.[7]

Theologians have added their voices to this investigation of the charm of our earthly home. Sally McFague describes the enchantment of this world when she writes of an "appreciation for the unbelievably vast, old, rich, diverse, and surprising cosmos, of which one's self is an infinitesimal but conscious part, the part able to sing its praises."[8] Wendy Farley comments: "The world . . . is good in and for itself even with its hardships. The world is also an opening, a sacrament of something beyond itself. The world is both itself and a doorway to the Divine Eros."[9]

"Children of the Light"

August 21, 2017: a solar eclipse transits the United States. A thousand years ago this sight would have caused great alarm, even terror. A world gone dark; the sun in all its force and reliability extinguished at mid-day. People everywhere saw this as a portent or worse—the beginning of the end of the life they had known and trusted for years.

Since then, we sophisticated modern people have learned what eclipses are about. We have educated ourselves in the celestial mechanics that orchestrate such heavenly displays. We know that what occurs is simply part of a universe running on its own laws, planets and moon and sun crisscrossing the sky with the occasional coincidence. Nothing to be alarmed about. And yet.

As the eclipse of August 2017 approached, millions dropped whatever they were doing and grabbed flimsy plastic glasses to observe this brief drama in the sky. To watch the darkened sun, if only for a moment, triggered something in many that was close to awe. A columnist in the *New York Times* observed, "it is hard, no matter how enlightened you consider yourself to be, not to feel a primordial lurch in your gut when the sun suddenly disappears from the sky." Because "we are children of the light," the maximum eclipse when the corona of the sun appears will evoke for many "a hidden vibration in your soul, the intuition of something seen. . . ."[10] This is what Ricoeur means by a *second naïveté.*

A thousand years ago, Jews and Christians saluted the display of a rainbow at the end of a storm as a sacred sign.

They remembered God's promise in the Bible that the universal deluge that ended life for those not on Noah's ark would never be repeated. To keep this promise, God would intervene in nature to broadcast a rainbow signaling the end of a storm. "I have set my rainbow in the clouds and it shall be a sign of the covenant between me and the earth" (Genesis 9:12).

When Isaac Newton devised an experiment that refracted light into the spectrum of colors that humans had seen in the celestial rainbow, it became clear that rainbows were utterly natural. God's intervention was not on display here. Beliefs we had cherished for centuries now seemed more than suspect. Scientific demonstration was replacing religious understandings of how the world works.

Schooled in the ways of science we still find ourselves delighted by a rainbow. The beauty and timing of this sudden epiphany still feels like a gift: light following storm. Here too we are in the realm of what Paul Ricoeur calls a *second naïveté*.

Charles Taylor names the natural wonder at our world—the enchantment—that survives scientific and sophisticated explanations of our universe. "The wonder is not only at the stupendous whole, but at the way in which we emerge, in one way fragile and insignificant, and yet capable of grasping the whole." There is a spirituality imbedded in these emotions. "One can even say that a kind of piety arises here, in which we recognize that for all our detachment in objectifying thought, we ultimately belong to this whole, and return to it." [11]

Pope Francis, in his encyclical letter on the environment, adds his voice to this exploration of a spirituality of the world. "From panoramic vistas to the tiniest living form, nature is a constant source of wonder and awe. It is also a continuing revelation of the divine." [12]

Many today experience a deep dissatisfaction with lives that seem empty of any larger purpose. Their search, often described as "spiritual but not religious," is too often mocked as superficial or new age. But, as Taylor writes, "these people are seeking a kind of unity and wholeness of the self, a reclaiming of the place of feeling, against a one-sided pre-eminence of reason, and a reclaiming of the body and its pleasures from the inferior and often guilt-ridden place it had been allowed in the disciplined, instrumental identity."[13]

Transcendence Within, Not Beyond

People were pestering Jesus about the belief that the reign of God would soon descend from on high to transform their world. Jesus assured them that this belief was not some distant ideal, that, in fact, the reign of God was already arriving in every act of mercy and justice. This ancient ideal was not waiting to descend from the heavens; nor did it exist in some transcendent realm. It was, in the famous formula, already and not yet. Nor was it a hope that thrived only within individuals' hearts. The Greek of the New Testament makes its communal character clear: "the kingdom of God is *among you*" (Luke 17:21).

Despite this emphasis on the earthly present, the early Christians could not resist looking heavenward in expectation of new revelations. In their cosmology, heaven existed high above this messy world, as surely as hell awaited in some fiery subterranean domain. If this cosmology perished with modern understandings of the cosmos, Christians have been slow to reimagine transcendence—the utter beyondness of their God—as a mysterious enchantment abiding within our one reality.

"Transcendence is not merely what lies beyond the world, but first and foremost what supports its givenness." Louis Dupré describes the tectonic shift still taking place in the Christian imagination. The awesome world we find ourselves in, whose origins and purposes we cannot account for, offers clues to a transcendent reality that envelopes and sustains us. This is the *givenness* of the world: an in-your-face astonishment that both confounds and enchants. The effort to fathom this *givenness* continues as an attempt "to revise the accepted idea of transcendence in a way that transform[s] the concept of a power hierarchically transmitted from *beyond* into a source of power *within* the universe whereby God's presence permeate[s] all parts at once."[14] This abundance of life—all there is before us, around us, among us—is the meaning of transcendence.

The Second Naïveté of Miracles

Christian authors from Charles Taylor and Pope Francis to novelist Marilynne Robinson describe the miracle of the world we are fortunate enough to inhabit. The English word "miracle"—so central a part of traditional Christian faith—is a relatively late arrival to the story of salvation. In the Greek of the New Testament Jesus's healing actions were most often rendered as "mighty works" or "deeds of power." The Gospel of Mark tells us that in his hometown Jesus's lineage was too well known and as a result "he could do no mighty works" (Mark 6:5; King James translation [KJV]). In the modern New American Standard translation, "mighty works" was replaced by the English word "miracles." In the yet more recent New Revised Standard Version (NRSV) translators have returned to the more literal phrase, "Jesus could do no deeds of power."

The English term *miracle* arose at a time—between the KJV in the early 1600s and the recent NRSV—when Christians were picturing the world in a severely dualistic fashion: nature meant the physical world with its laws of force and motion; this was the domain of science and reason. Transcendent to this material world was the realm of the supernatural. In such a divided reality a miracle came to mean an act of God intervening into the otherwise ordinary world of physical laws and facts. Such miracles were, by definition, *unnatural.* Charles Taylor describes this "modern concept of the 'miracle' [as] a kind of punctual hole blown in the regular order of things from outside, that is, from the transcendent." Miracles, like God's grace, seemed to belong to another supernatural world. Our own darkened world, if lit at all, must be illumined by a divine light from a great distance.

Taylor suggests an interpretation of miracle that better fits the *second naïveté* of Paul Ricoeur. "Belonging to the earth, the sense of our dark genesis, can also be part of Christian faith . . . it is perhaps precisely the ordinary operation of things which constitute the 'miracle.'" (He must place the word "miracle" in quotes to indicate this new usage.)[15]

In her novel *Gilead* Marilynne Robinson provides an example of one generation's experience of miraculous visions being replaced by a later generation's experience of miraculous, healing memories. John Ames, writing to his young son, recalls how his own grandfather, also a minister, had spoken of the visions in which the Lord would appear to him. "When I was a young man the Lord came to me and put His hand here on my right shoulder. . . . I would call that experience a vision. We had visions in those days, a number of us did."[16]

Ames realizes that his own life was not privileged with such supernatural visitations. Yet for him something simi-

lar to these visions comes to him in certain sacred memories. He returns to just such a memory of the time that a
church had been struck by lightning and had burned to the
ground. Families from the area gathered to pull down the
remains of the building and rescue a few Bibles and hym-
nals that had survived the fire. Ames remembers the men
who were working in the ashes of the church and how the
ash turned into mush in the rain. He remembers his father
bringing him a biscuit that had soot on it. When the boy
seemed bothered by the ash, his father assured him, "Never
mind . . . there's nothing cleaner than ash." In his memory,
bread and ash mingle and are accompanied by a powerful
sense of communion. "I remember it as communion, and I
believe that's what it was." [17]

Some cherished memories return as miraculous revelations. Memory itself, at the edge of our consciousness and
not always under our bidding, transfigures the ordinary
to reveal and "sanctify" the everyday as exceptional. Robinson's example of a sooty biscuit received as communion
reiterates her conviction that sacredness appears in the most
ordinary parts of life. Now, when Ames holds a Bible in his
hand, he often recalls that scene at the destroyed church
building, and the Bible "is somehow sanctified by that
memory." The sacred book does not sanctify the memory
but quite the opposite: the memory makes holy the Bible.

The charming world that Ames's grandfather had inhabited (enjoying direct communication with the Lord) was no
more, but another kind of enchantment had survived. Memories of ashen biscuits become spiritual communion testify
to a world still open to enchantment. Paul Ricoeur would
describe the elder Ames's literal visions in terms of a *primitive naïveté*, an immediacy of belief, now lost. But in its place
Robinson and Ames, in a *second naïveté*, find another kind of

enchanting vision. Spiritual "visions" continue to exist, now enrobed in compelling memories.

Elsewhere, Robinson seconds Taylor's appreciation of the miraculous—that is, the enchanted nature of the world of which we are a part. "Nothing could be more miraculous than the fact that we have a consciousness that makes the world intelligible to us and are moved by what is beautiful."[18] To some Christians this use of "miracle" may seem to empty the term of its supernatural richness; to others it speaks to our recognition that the first and most enduring miracle is creation itself.

Resources

1. Paul Ricoeur, *The Symbolism of Evil*, 349. Ricoeur's imagery traces cultural change from a *primitive naïveté*, when religious belief was simple, through centuries of scientific and cultural changes, often experienced by Christians as "a desert of criticism," to a new stage of belief that he entitles a *second naïveté*.

2. Taylor, *A Secular Age*, 26.

3. Louis Dupré, *Passage to Modernity: An Essay in the Hermeneutics of Nature and Culture* (New Haven, CT: Yale University Press, 1993), 3.

4. Ricoeur, *The Symbolism of Evil*, 349.

5. Jill Lepore quotes Carson's *Silent Spring* in her essay "The Shorebird," *The New Yorker*, March 26, 2018, 72.

6. Rachel Carson, *The Edge of the Sea* (Boston: Houghton Mifflin, 1955), 4, 7, 250.

7. See Lepore's "The Shorebird," 72.

8. Sallie McFague, *The Body of God* (Minneapolis: Fortress Press, 1993), 112.

9. Wendy Farley, *The Wounding and Healing of Desire* (Louisville, KY: Westminster John Knox Press, 2005), 13.

10. Dennis Overbye, "During an Eclipse, Darkness Falls, Wonder Rises," *New York Times*, August 15, 2017, D3.

11. Taylor, *A Secular Age*, 607.

12. Pope Francis, *Laudato Si'*; §85; the pope is quoting from a document written by the Canadian Conference of Catholic Bishops.

13. Taylor, *A Secular Age,* 507.

14. Dupré, *Passage to Modernity,* 252. The emphasis is ours.

15. Taylor, *A Secular Age,* 547.

16. Robinson, *Gilead,* 175.

17. Ibid., 96.

18. Robinson writes about the miraculous in "The Art of Fiction No. 198," quoted in Paul Lakeland, *The Wounded Angel: Fiction and the Religious Imagination* (Collegeville, MN: Liturgical Press, 2017), 200.

PART THREE

Imagination Enchanted

Faith is the living out of the figures of hope unleashed by the imagination. —Paul Ricoeur

Christians differ about the central avenue of their religious enchantment: Creation itself or the Cross of Christ. Each illumines a distinctive path through which we approach the gracious enchantment of our days.

The life journey of Christians—and all of creation—is captured in the image of the Communion of Saints.

The common experience of time as a chronic unfolding of life to death can be reimagined and even enchanted by the biblical encouragement to redeem the time.

CHAPTER NINE

The Virtuous Imagination

The discipline of reality is nothing without the grace of imagination.

Paul Ricoeur

ENCHANTMENT EMERGES first in the forge of the imagination. The intriguing person we have just encountered lingers in memory, remaining vibrant in imagination. The music that has just captured our attention likewise lingers, beguiling and enchanting us. And religious faith stirs in this same precinct. "Faith is the living out of the figures of hope unleashed by the imagination."[1] All this is imagination as enchantment.

If the imagination is difficult to define, its works are most familiar to us. The monster under the small child's bed is, of course, lurking in his imagination. The Harry Potter books have flooded the imaginations of the world's young with many fantastic but appealing creatures. Theologian Craig Dykstra writes, "The human imagination is the integrating process that provides linkage between ourselves and the world—and within ourselves, between our bodies, minds and emotions, our very souls and spirits. It is by means of the imagination that we are able to come really to 'see' and understand anything at all—even, in a sense, to 'see' God."[2]

Centuries earlier Thomas Aquinas offered his estimation of the importance of imagination: "The image is the principle of our knowledge. It is that from which the intellectual activity begins, not as a passing stimulus, but as an enduring foundation. When the imagination is choked, so also is our theological knowledge."[3]

Cultivating the Imagination

In Christian history the imagination was often seen as the source of sexual temptations and angry fantasies. Erotic dreams, waking and sleeping, had their source in the imagination. It was also in the imagination that people would play out fantasies of violence—striking back at an enemy or cruelly punishing an adversary. Thus did this interior resource gain a reputation as the devil's workshop.

Quite apart from moral considerations of sex and violence, the imagination seemed to play a dangerous game: from this interior theater sprang fantastic images of unicorns and aliens from fictitious planets; the imagination seemed to relish fabricating and even distorting reality. Such play might be allowed in the make-believe world of the child, but with adult maturity we surely should set aside such irresponsible diversions and bind ourselves to the dictates of reason and duty. How could the fruits of imagination—so often frivolous or even dangerous—contribute to a virtuous life?

So it was that the imagination came to be seen as a rogue faculty, a wild card in the interior life. The rehabilitation of emotion in recent decades[4]—the recognition that emotions are cognitive and more than hormonal surges—has opened the door to an appreciation of imagination as a wondrous if volatile power waiting to be cultivated so that it may move us toward our best hopes and deepest values.

If today we are more positively disposed to the gifts of

imagination, we also recognize how this capacity can be neutered. Individuals whose lives are submerged in routines of work or distraction are likely to numb their imagination until its native energy is all but lost. A cautiousness too well learned can also shut down this interior resource.

The imagination is likewise hijacked by compulsiveness. When a person becomes absorbed by a concern, an ideal, or a fantasy, these may come to utterly capture his imagination; the person is unable to think of anything else. Whether it is rage and the desire for revenge, whether it is a sexual fantasy that dominates the mind, whether it is a worry that will not subside, the imagination is made hostage to a repetitive rumination. Obsessions and addictions enthrall this interior resource so that it no longer serves the common good of the whole person. In our social lives, fundamentalism and racism wound our imagination, freezing it with stereotypes that leave us closed to new information about others. This categorizing of others leads, inevitably, away from compassion toward injustice and even violence.

The reclaiming of imagination as a healthy resource both in civic and religious life begins in a recognition that the virtues of empathy and compassion spring from this interior domain. In imagination we entertain not only fantasies of violence and revenge but also hopeful scenarios of healing and reconciliation. The virtue of compassion, in which we are moved by the misery and vulnerability of others, has its roots in imagination. Imagination, if often unruly or simply bewildering, plays an essential role in a life that would grow more loving and just.

Two philosophers have given us a richer appreciation of the cultivation of the imagination. Paul Ricoeur reminds us that knowledge itself is not a simple recording of a stable reality. We do not merely record what we behold; instead, the human mind is always assembling, editing, and reimagining the many facets of the world with which it is confronted. "We invent in order to discover; we exert energy in making meanings so as to apprehend the character of our existence and our world."[5] Paintings and poems, sonnets and hymns are inventions that would unveil enchantments half glimpsed. The fully human world of meaning and value is a world both discovered and created. And in the labor of its creation we see the powerful role of imagination and, in fortunate moments, undergo its charms.

Philosopher Martha Nussbaum suggests that as a child listens to nursery rhymes, she is alerted to wonder—"a sense of mystery that mingles curiosity with awe." This opening of the imagination to the lives of others helps the child recognize in fables and fairy tales the range of emotions she is discovering in herself. "The habits of wonder promoted by storytelling thus define the other person as spacious and deep, with qualitative differences from oneself and hidden places worthy of respect."[6]

This is the beginning of empathy and a path to enchantment. In imagination we cross over from our world of feeling into that of another person; in this exercise we are not engulfed or overwhelmed by their feelings but are able to identify with the powerful affect in another. We recognize that people who seem so different from us also have "hidden places worthy of respect." From these early realizations will flower, with proper cultivation, both the virtue of compassion and opportunities for relationships that will enrich our lives.

The Theater of the Imagination

Imagination is more than a private resource. In a theater we have the opportunity to envision the lives of other persons.

Playwright David Mamet discusses the peculiar healing effect of good drama on the imagination. "We have, through following the course of the drama, left aside, for two hours, the delusion that we are powerful and wise, and we leave the theater better for the rest."[7]

The imagination is a transformative power: it allows us to re-envision our social world and to picture alternatives to the status quo. Nobel laureate Seamus Heaney argues, in a similar vein, that "the nobility of poetry . . . is the imagination pressing back against the pressure of reality." And he suggests that "poetry's high potential [is] its function as an agent of possible transformation, of an evolution toward the more radiant and generous life which the imagination desires."[8]

"The Imagination Is the Scout of the Will"

The transformative power of the imagination appears in its ability to question lessons we have learned from our civic and religious upbringing. Roberto Unger writes, "Though society informs these lessons it does not inform them entirely. The unshaped part—the deviations, the anomalies, the surprises—provides the visionary imagination with the materials for subversive insight."[9]

In a more recent work, Unger broadens the lens of his analysis to examine the social tension of our lives as necessarily contextualized by institutions and ideologies, yet able to transcend these limiting frameworks. Much of the work of an institution, such as the Catholic Church, is undertaken *within the framework* of the organization—a framework that we take for granted. In such an institutional structure, many established policies go unchallenged or even unnoticed. But on occasion, questions arise *about the organizational framework* itself. Such questions may well provoke an institutional crisis. Unger observes that "only when there is a crisis—that is to say, a problem for which the established structure offers no ready-made solution—do we hit against the limits of our present ideas and methods." It is at such a point, an impasse, that an organization may become open to the prophetic imagination.

In a time of great cultural change, an institution must "be able to make moves it never made before, according to rules it can formulate, if at all, only after making them." This prospect can be terrifying for an institution that is wedded to historical precedent, but it is crucial for survival in the face of social upheaval. Unger notes that at such critical moments in an organization's life, imagination works like "a scout of the will," suggesting creative strategies for getting from here to there. An institution such as the church need not wait for a severe crisis to initiate reform. "The imagination does the work of crisis without crisis, making it possible for us to experience change without undergoing ruin." [10]

Prophecy and Imagination

Imagination played a starring role in the development of the Bible. Our earliest religious ancestors imagined our beginnings as taking place in an enchanted garden. Their stories of deserts, oases, and exile, of a place "flowing with milk and honey," provided the Christian tradition with ready-made metaphors of threat and hope. Biblical scholar Walter Brueggemann defines biblical revelation as "an act of faithful imagination that buoyantly and defiantly mediates a counterworld that is a wondrous demanding alternative to the world immediately and visibly at hand." [11]

Prophets in the Jewish tradition entertained in their imaginations a reality that did not yet exist. Isaiah's vision of "swords beaten into plowshares" (Isaiah 2:4) existed first only in his imagination, and if it still abides largely in hope, it manages to motivate today those committed to a more peaceful world. Jesus continued in this tradition of prophets, foreseeing a reality that was already and not yet. "The reign of God is among you" (Luke 17:21).

In the course of the third century, as church leaders sought to consolidate the various memories of the first generations of Christians, a consensus grew that God's revelation was now complete. No new revelations were to be awaited. Certain books—the four Gospels, Paul's letters—would now be considered the sole legitimate versions of Christian revelation. With revelation supposedly complete, obedience to this received wisdom would replace any need for further prophecies. And so prophecy—and with it the play of the religious imagination—began to wither in the Christian tradition. Prophecy, of course, did not utterly disappear but was pushed to the margins of the faith, now stirring in the fertile imaginations of mystics and heretics.

In recent years, biblical scholars have been reclaiming the active role of imagination in faith itself, and this has brought a renewed interest in the gift of prophecy. Again Brueggemann: "It is the vocation of the prophet to keep alive the ministry of imagination, to keep on conjuring and proposing alternative futures to the single one the king wants to urge as the only thinkable one." He reminds us that "the task of prophetic ministry is to nurture, nourish, and evoke a consciousness and perception alternative to the consciousness and perception of the dominant culture around us." [12]

Prophets help communities of faith see through the present, to recognize God's action breaking into our lives. The present—all the duties, delights, and distractions that fill our days—naturally absorbs our attention. The good we are doing and the troubles we are facing conspire to consume us.

Our daily duties, faithfully repeated, become the status quo. "This is how we do it around here" gradually morphs into "this is the right way, the only way to do things." Finally the status quo becomes something like what we might call a royal arrangement. Prophets help a community pierce the veil of the present and reckon with something novel that is stirring. "Behold, I am doing a new thing. Now it springs forth. Do you not perceive it?" (Isaiah 43:19).

The Bible Tutors the Imagination

Moral theologian Bill Spohn has explored how the moral effect of Scripture is largely on the imagination. The Bible, he argues, does not simply tell us what to do in each instance. Instead, its imaginative stories and symbols "encourage certain scenarios." These vignettes—Jesus repeatedly conversing with sinners, or asking his disciples to forgive seventy times seven, or his healing the sick—"become scenarios for action by evoking affective energies in distinctive ways." Faith is an energy that ignites affective energies of compassion and hope, just as faith stirs the imagination to see the world in new ways. When we return to these stories again and again we are bathing our imaginations in a distinct vision of reality. The role of the Bible, with its dramatic parables and compelling images, is to "tutor the imagination."[13]

Religious faith is a way of imagining the world. Believing that our world was created by and is now sustained by a loving creator who is present yet invisible takes a strong imagination. This is not to suggest that faith is a fantasy or a mere figment of our mind. It is to recognize that religious belief is a God-given capacity to picture the world in a particular and powerful fashion.

When imagination becomes a virtuous resource in our spiritual life we are able to see the disparate events of our past as part of a plot, a vocation with direction and purpose. Through the prism of inspired imagination deserts and exiles are refashioned into graceful way stations on a miraculous journey.

With imagination we also make sense of present distress—the impasses that mark the journey today. Through the prism of imagination our sorrow is reframed into graceful grieving rather than toxic resentment.

And with imagination we even envision an extraordinary future, a time reshaped by justice and compassion, a season when we begin to detect flickering indications of the coming reign of God.

Resources

1. Paul Ricoeur, *Figuring the Sacred* (Minneapolis, MN: Augsburg Fortress Press, 1995), 8. The epigram at the beginning of the chapter is from Ricoeur's *Freud and Philosophy* (New Haven, CT: Yale University Press, 1970), 551.

2. Craig Dykstra, "Pastoral and Ecclesial Imagination," in *For Life Abundant* (Grand Rapids, MI: Eerdmans, 2008), 49.

3. See Thomas Aquinas, *Opusculum* 16, in *De trinitate* 6,2, ad 5; this judgment is quoted in Margaret Miles, *Image as Insight* (Boston: Beacon Press, 1985), 142.

4. Martha Nussbaum has led this recovery of the cognitive quality of emotions. See her *Upheavals of Thought: The Intelligence of Emotions* (Cambridge: Cambridge University Press, 2001).

5. William Schweiker quotes Ricoeur in his essay "Understanding Moral Meanings: On Philosophical Hermeneutics and Theological Ethics," in *Christian Ethics, Problems and Prospects*, ed. Lisa Sowle Cahill and James F. Childress (Cleveland, OH: Pilgrim Press, 1996), 78.

6. Martha Nussbaum, *Cultivating Humanity* (Cambridge, MA: Harvard University Press, 1997), 90.

7. David Mamet, "Attention Must Be Paid," *New York Times*, February 13, 2005, 13.

8. Seamus Heaney, *The Redress of Poetry* (New York: Farrar, Straus and Giroux, 1996), 114.

9. Unger, *Passion*, 149.

10. Unger, *The Awakened Self* (Cambridge, MA: Harvard University Press, 2007). The quotations are from pp. 125, 112, and 68 respectively.

11. Walter Brueggemann, "Imaginative Remembering," in *An Introduction to the Old Testament* (Louisville, KY: Westminster John Knox, 2003), 26.

12. Walter Brueggemann, *The Prophetic Imagination* (Philadelphia: Fortress Press, 1978), 13, 45.

13. William Spohn, "Jesus and Christian Ethics," *Theological Studies* 56 (1995): 104.

CHAPTER TEN

Creation and the Cross— Wellsprings of Enchantment

The art of living is more about wrestling than dancing.
Marcus Aurelius

MARCUS AURELIUS, Stoic philosopher whose day job was emperor of Rome, described two styles of embrace: one more romantic and possibly enchanting; the other more combative, a necessary stance in a hostile, disenchanted world. These two embraces resonate with two Christian spiritualities, two visions of the world and God's enchanting presence within it. One is more optimistic; the other, more pessimistic. One is more enthusiastic; the other, more sober. Each spirituality, firmly rooted in Scripture, is genuinely Christian. Their differences name some of the tensions in Christian life today.

These two streams of spirituality emerged early in our tradition as they sponsored different visions of sacred enchantment. Their paths would sometimes intermingle, reinforce each other, and move in harmony; at other times they would diverge and become mutually challenging if not threatening avenues of belief and practice. Both spiritualities—the more optimistic and the more pessimistic—can quote chapter and verse in Scripture to defend their vision of Christian life.

No doubt, each orientation was also powerfully influenced by lived experience. In times of social disorder—of war or famine—or personal histories of poverty or illness, Christians would find themselves wrestling with the troubles and dangers in life. The theologies of Augustine and Luther illustrate such a response. At other times and in other circumstances—periods of peace and of collective well-being—Christians would be more inclined to an optimistic view of their surrounding culture and its compatibility with their faith. The work of Thomas Aquinas and Karl Rahner exhibit this more positive view of the world.

The year 180 of the Common Era stands as an intriguing point where these optimistic and pessimistic worldviews crossed paths. At that time Irenaeus, the bishop of Lyons, wrote that "the glory of God is a human person fully alive."[1] That God's transcendent glory shines out of a human person, despite the person's frailty, points to a vision of this world as already enchanted. At the same time Marcus Aurelius, not a Christian but a Stoic philosopher, gave expression to the more sober worldview: "the art of living is more about wrestling than dancing."[2] In this orientation the enchantment of God's grace must be contested, finally wrested away from a broken and disenchanted environment.

Theologian Catherine Hilkert contrasts the role of imagination in these conflicting visions of enchantment:

> The sacramental imagination ... emphasizes the presence of the God who is self-communicating love, the creation of human beings in the image of God (restless hearts seeking the divine), the mystery of the incarnation. ...

Hilkert then describes the characteristics of a more adversarial vision:

The dialectical imagination stresses the distance between God and humanity, the hiddenness and absence of God, the sinfulness of human beings, the paradox of the cross. . . .[3]

The Christian spirituality that flows from a sacramental imagination sees the world itself as a sign of God's presence: the beauty and wonder of nature are always and already enchanted with the charm of its creator, just as every human creature, in all their brokenness, may become a sacrament or sign, in Irenaeus's imagery, of "the glory of God." This spirituality is rooted in the Incarnation: the Word become flesh has made the human body and our sensual lives themselves into enchanting sacraments of grace.

This highly optimistic worldview is opposed to a spirituality that has a more "dialectical" or adversarial view of the world. In this second orientation, Christians bring a more cautious and suspicious eye to the world. In this spirituality believers emphasize the rupture in creation. Though the world is God's creation, violence and sin now stalk human society, and self-deception has profoundly injured human nature. This worldview recognizes the pandemic of corruption and injustice so evident throughout human society. We can glimpse the stark contrast of these two spiritual orientations if we examine their different starting points.

Creation or the Cross

The spirituality that flows from a sacramental imagination begins with creation. This worldview celebrates all creatures and nature itself as glorious witnesses of God's own beauty and abundance. This spirituality finds signs of abundant grace throughout creation—even our sensual lives become places where grace abounds.

CREATION AND THE CROSS:
WELLSPRINGS OF ENCHANTMENT

A Sacramental Imagination	*A Dialectical Imagination*
Emphasizes harmony of	Emphasizes tension between
God and the world	God and the world
Grace and nature	Grace and nature
Spirit and flesh	Spirit and flesh

STARTING POINT

Creation	The cross

THE WORLD

God's creation: filled with delight and grace	Hostile to holiness; not our final home

THE CHURCH

Sacrament to the world	Sanctuary of the saved

SPIRITUALITY

Engagement	Detachment
Presence	Absence
Abundance	Scarcity
Feasting	Fasting

Figure One

See Catherine Hilkert's *Naming Grace* (New York: Continuum, 1997), 15; and David Tracy's *Analogical Imagination* (New York: Crossroad, 1981), 405–55.

The spirituality that flows from a dialectical imagination begins with the cross of Jesus Christ and humankind's need of redemption. This orientation begins with the painful memory of the Fall and all the sin and disharmony that flowed from that original failure. This spirituality sponsors a more sober and suspicious view of the disenchanted world in which we live. Suffering takes center stage, replacing the humanistic enthusiasm of the other spirituality. This worldview is likewise more cautious about the body and its passions, keenly aware of how often humans are led astray by their selfish desires. The cross—ordinary wood—becomes enchanted as the crucifix, locus of Jesus's death and the beginning of our salvation.

The difference between these two spiritual orientations becomes clearer when we compare their attitude toward "the world" (*kosmos* in the Greek of the New Testament). The more pessimistic spirituality endorses the many negative judgments in John's Gospel about the world as a dangerous and ungodly place. In this Gospel, Jesus often cautions his disciples: "The world hates me because I testify against it that its works are evil" (John 7). Jesus tells his disciples, "I have chosen you out of the world . . . therefore the world hates you" (John 15). And then, most emphatically in his final hours, "my kingdom is not of this world" (John 18).

This negative view of "the world" becomes even stronger in the First Letter of John: "Do not love the world or the things of the world" (1 John 2). The only good thing about the world, in this view, is that it is coming to an end; "the world and its desires are passing away." This is a world that distracts Christians from the love of God; it is a place where Satan holds sway. Here human cultures and secular society are seen as ungodly and likely to seduce people away from virtuous living. From this spirituality grew the caution concerning the triple threat to holiness: "the world, the flesh, and the devil." Historian Peter Brown, in *The Body and Society*, notes that St. Paul used "the world" and "the flesh" as a kind of shorthand to refer to the worst behaviors sponsored by society and our own embodied selves. But this was a dangerous usage; later readers would be tempted to take these words literally and see both human bodies and secular society as already and thoroughly corrupt.[4]

Elsewhere in the Gospels we find a very different view of the world. The world itself is the scene of the Incarnation: this is where God has chosen to dwell in the flesh. It is in John's Gospel, the site of an otherwise pessimistic view of "the world," that we read of the Word made flesh and where we are reminded: "For God so loved the world that he gave his only son so that everyone who believed in him may not perish but may have eternal life" (John 3). When Jesus told his followers that "the reign of God is among you" (Luke 17:21), he meant here in this world at every moment. In the more optimistic spirituality the world is not something to be abandoned but precisely a reality that awaits redemption. St. Paul describes God's plan of salvation: "In Christ, God is reconciling the world to God" (2 Corinthians 5:19).

Critics of the more pessimistic spirituality argue that a turn away from "the world" means a disengagement that borders on irresponsibility. If a Christian is convinced that the world holds no lasting value (since "it is passing away" and heaven is our only true home), then this person will have little motivation to contribute to the healing of nature and the moral transformation of society. A Christian disengagement from history contributed, many have argued, to the Western vision of "nature" as something to be used and plundered rather than reverenced.

What Is the Church For?

Does the Christian Church serve as a beacon, casting its illumination and warmth throughout the world, or is it meant to be a sanctuary in a hostile world? The more optimistic spirituality sees the Christian church as itself a sacrament or sign of God's loving presence in the world. The Vatican II document on the church opens with this conviction. "Since the Church, in Christ, is a sacrament—a sign and instrument, that is, of communion with God and of the unity of the entire human race. . . ."[5] If Christ is the light of the world, then the community of his followers might expect to transmit that enchanting illumination to the larger society. In this spirituality the church's purpose lies beyond itself. It is not an institution that should focus most of its energy on self-survival and defense.

A more pessimistic spirituality pictures the Christian church with very different metaphors. This worldview endorses the scriptural memory of the church as a saving ark ("the barque of Peter"). The church is like the ship that saved Noah and his family and the animals he brought on board from the great flood. In these images, the church is pictured as the unique place of salvation: only these few passengers will be saved; all others are predestined for drowning. Here the church becomes a sanctuary in a hostile world.

Salvation—Abundant or Scarce?

The more sober spirituality has traditionally pictured eternal salvation as a gift of God promised especially to "the chosen people"—first, the Jews, and then, Christians. Many Christians, reading St. Paul's words about those whom

God has chosen to save ("those whom he predestined, he also called," Romans 8:30), came to believe that the gift of salvation was scarce. Salvation was offered only to those who explicitly believed in Jesus Christ. All others—unfortunately—would not be saved. The New Testament seemed clear on this point. "The one who believes and is baptized will be saved; but the one who does not believe will be condemned" (Mark 16:16). "There is no other name under heaven given among men by which we must be saved" (Acts of the Apostles 4:12).

The more optimistic spirituality assumes a very different view of redemption. Salvation is here pictured in a more extravagant fashion as believers remember the New Testament conviction, "God our savior who desires everyone to be saved and to come to the knowledge of the truth . . ." (1 Timothy 2:4). Followers of this spirituality also remember the prayer at Pentecost: "Send forth your Spirit and it will renew the face of the earth." The hope is not just for individual Christians, but for a renewal of *the face of the earth*. All creation is included in God's economy of salvation.

Karl Rahner has been an outspoken proponent of this hopeful spiritual orientation. "The salvation of an individual does not consist in escaping from the history of humanity but in entering into that history's absolute future, which we call 'the Kingdom of God.'" Rahner argues that salvation is not a gift reserved only for those in the church. "Salvation is achieved not only within the explicitly religious sphere but in all dimensions of human existence, i.e., where man does not interpret his actions in a consciously religious way, but where he loves in an absolutely responsible manner. . . ."[6]

The documents of Vatican II support this broader view of salvation: "We ought to believe that the Holy Spirit in a manner known only to God offers to every person the possibility of salvation" (*Gaudium et Spes*, §22). Such a view includes a vision of the Holy Spirit operating throughout time and space: "The Holy Spirit was already at work in the world before Christ was glorified" (*Ad Gentes*, §4).

This vision of salvation—as a gift not reserved for a privileged few but offered to all mankind and in some way including the universe itself—expands the meaning of salvation history. God's plan of salvation is now seen as including the entire universe. Theologian Thomas O'Meara writes:

> The history of salvation is the history of grace present in all history, as God's special action towards us over and beyond our creation as men and women. The history of salvation includes all the world's religions. They do not exist apart from salvation history.[7]

The history of salvation points to an enchanting transformation that is already under way. The Christian liturgy is not a collection of rites removed from the world but a ritual enactment of what is always taking place through human history, what Rahner calls "the liturgy of the world."[8]

Vital Traditions; Enduring Tensions

The enduring vitality of the Christian tradition is seen in the rich complexity of its belief: Christians confess that Jesus Christ is both human and divine. This belief creates an unavoidable tension; for two thousand years believers have been trying to say more clearly and more convincingly what this mystery could mean. It is to be expected that in one era Christ's divine identity would be more emphasized; at another time Jesus's humanity would receive greater attention.

So it is with the tension between God's grace and human effort. Christians believe it is God's grace alone that makes life and forgiveness possible. But humans must cooperate with this grace; we are not passive victims, but active participants in our salvation.

So it is with the relation of faith and culture. Christians have long been convinced that their beliefs require them to stand against unhealthy tendencies in the surrounding culture, whether these concern injustice or idolatry. The tradition calls for a certain detachment. Yet Christians are called to participate in the culture as well; they are citizens as well as religious believers. In the depth of their exile the ancient Jews heard the call of Jeremiah: "Seek the welfare (*shalom*) of the city where I have sent you into exile. And pray to the Lord on its behalf, for in its welfare you will find your welfare" (Jeremiah 29:7). If Christian spirituality demands detachment, it also requires attachment. After all, our commitments and our fidelity are attachments that bind us to God and one another.

Trouble arises when one spirituality—whether it be the more sober or the more enthusiastic—comes to dominate Christian faith, and a healthy tension begins to wither. Then the more sober spirituality, become dominant, will not only criticize the surrounding culture but find it totally devoid of God's grace. Religious belief will become not only countercultural, as it must always be, but anticultural, severing itself from the surrounding environment. Or the more enthusiastic spirituality, become dominant, will begin to so immerse itself in the surrounding culture that it loses its prophetic edge and its unique identity. It becomes little more than a "civil religion." The vitality of the tradition survives in its healthy tensions.

So the challenge will always be both to recognize the

presence of God among humankind and to honor God's painful absence. The tension arises in the realization that God is never fully present nor completely absent. Instead, as the Scriptures testify again and again, God's presence is most often experienced as an epiphany: we see in a privileged moment—be that of bliss or suffering—the face of God in our lives. But this is a presence we cannot guarantee; God is too much of a transcendent mystery for us to manage such control.

Christian faith insists that God's abiding presence throughout creation renders this world enchanted. We celebrate this graceful charm of the world when we summon the enchantment of prayer, gesture, and song in our sacraments and other ceremonies. There will be seasons, in individual lives and cultural moments, when this enchantment seems to disappear. Often this is due to webs of disenchantment that our kind has woven into creation. So the endless challenge of uniting in our lives the double embrace described by Marcus Aurelius: to dance the abundant charm of God's world and to wrestle with the obstacles that have rendered our home, for the moment, disenchanted.

Resources

1. See Mary Ann Donovan, "Alive to the Glory of God: A Key Insight in St. Irenaeus," *Theological Studies* 49 (1988): 283–97.

2. Marcus Aurelius, *Meditations*, 70. See the translation of G. M. A. Grube (New York: Bobbs-Merrill, 1963).

3. Catherine Hilkert, *Naming Grace* (New York: Continuum, 1997), 15. Hilkert's full description: "the need for grace as redemption and reconciliation, the limits and necessity for critique of any human project or institution including the church, and the not-yet character of the promised reign of God." Hilkert is commenting on David Tracy's discussion of these styles of religious imagination as either dialectical or analogical. See Tracy's *Analogical*

Imagination (New York: Crossroad, 1998), 415. Her description of the dialectical imagination continues, "grace as divinizing as well as forgiving, the mediating role of the church as sacrament of salvation in the world, and the 'foretaste' of the reign of God that is present in human community wherever God's reign of justice, peace and love is fostered."

4. Peter Brown, *The Body and Society: Men, Women, and Sexual Renunciation in Early Christianity* (New York: Columbia University Press, 1988), 276.

5. See p. 1 of *Lumen Gentium* (Light to the Nations), in *The Basic Sixteen Documents of Vatican II.* "We know that the whole creation has been groaning in labor pains until now . . ." (Romans 8:22).

6. See Karl Rahner's essay "Christian Humanism," in *Theological Investigations*, vol. 9 (New York: Seabury, 1976), 189.

7. Thomas O'Meara, "A History of Grace," in *A World of Grace* (Washington, DC: Georgetown University Press, 1995), 83.

8. Skelly, *Liturgy of the World*, 85.

CHAPTER ELEVEN

Enchanting the Journey: The Communion of Saints

"So great a cloud of witnesses"

Hebrews 12:1

THE COMMUNION OF SAINTS does not suggest a gathering of the elect nor a convention of the canonized. Instead, this charming image pictures a transgenerational pilgrimage of believers—the living and dead, the holy and the sinful— moving together through history into the mystery of God. The journey of faith is not an individual slog but an enchanting adventure in the company of the faithful departed.

The Catholic author Flannery O'Connor conjured a striking vision of this transhistorical journey. In the short story "Revelation," a woman looks up to the sky and envisions a bizarre procession of humans. She suddenly saw that "a vast horde of souls were rumbling toward heaven." This motley crew included "white trash clean for the first time in their lives, negroes in white robes," and "battalions of freaks and lunatics shouting and clapping and leaping like frogs." Looking closer, she saw, "bringing up the rear of this procession was a tribe of people whom she recognized at once as those who, like herself and Claude, had always had a little of everything and the God-given wit to use it."[1] This

139

last group—her own privileged kind—was moving with great dignity, and they were the only ones singing on key.

Catholic scholars today are returning to this engaging vision of solidarity: John Theil: "The Catholic notion of the communion of saints assumes that the living and the dead are bound together in a network of relationships as the one body of Christ."[2] Elizabeth Johnson adds, "The symbol [of the Communion of Saints] signifies the relationship flowing among an intergenerational company of persons profoundly touched by the sacred, sharing in the cosmic community of life which is also sacred."[3]

This belief acknowledges a solidarity across centuries and a resilience among Christians who have held to their faith through persecution and martyrdom. It envisions a vibrant unity formed by all those believers who have come before this generation as well as the generations of those as yet unborn who will continue to enliven this gathering. The Communion of Saints, Johnson concludes, "comes to birth in a river of holy lives through the centuries, a great crowd to which those confessing the creed today also belong, to which generations yet unborn are destined, and to which the natural world forms both matrix and partner."[4]

In Georges Bernanos's *The Diary of a Country Priest*, the priest asks a troubled woman, "Don't you ever despair?" She responds, "no," insisting that she identifies with all those in the world who are also suffering, many whose circumstances are more difficult than her own. "I think of all the people I don't know of like me—an' there's plenty of 'em, a wide world it is—beggars ploddin' through the rain, kiddies with no home, all the ailin' and the mad folk in the asylums cryin' to the moon, and plenty, plenty more." Her saving strategy: "I slip into the crowd of 'em, makin' myself small, and its not only the livin' but the dead as well who was sufferin' once, and those that are comin', an'll be suffering too." The voices of this multitude across history comes to her "like a great murmurin' sendin' me to sleep."[5]

When the priest receives the diagnosis of his terminal cancer, the news does not isolate him or fill him with self-pity. Instead, he recalls the many who are living out similar scenarios. "This very day hundreds, thousands of us perhaps, all over the world, will be dazed by a similar sentence." In the midst of this bad news, he feels the consolation of belonging to such a gathering.

For the priest, this spiritual belonging brings with it a sense of resilience. "But experience has also taught me that I have inherited from my mother, and no doubt from other poor women of our kind, a sort of endurance, which in the long run is almost unlimited, because it doesn't attempt to vie with pain, but slips within, makes of it a habit in some way; that is our strength."[6]

The social activist Dorothy Day repeatedly evoked the image of the Communion of Saints, especially its inclusion of the poor and dispossessed. She described how the Catholic Church "had come down through the centuries since the time of Peter" and "still held the allegiance of masses of people in all the cities where I had lived. They poured in and out of her doors on Sunday and holy days, her novenas and missions."[7]

Catholic philosopher Charles Taylor has sought to restore vitality to this ancient mystical sense: a visceral awareness of belonging to a heritage of saints and sinners who all together move through human history toward a shared destiny. He recalls the imagery of the poet Charles Peguy: "The sinner extends his hand to the saint, since the saint reaches out to help him. And all together, the one through the other, the one pulling the other, they form a chain that rises up to

Jesus, a chain of fingers that can't be disconnected. . . . The one who is not Christian is the one who does not offer his hand."[8]

Taylor comments: this is "not just as a communion of perfected persons, who have left their imperfections behind them; but rather as a communion of whole lives, of whole itineraries towards God. The whole itinerary is what we constantly retell in the lives of the saints." He adds, "My itinerary crucially includes my existence embedded in a historic order, with its good and bad, in and out of which I must move towards God's order. The [end time] must bring together all these itineraries, with their very different landscapes and perils."[9]

A Cosmic Communion of Saints

During one of the archaeological digs he participated in while living in China, the Jesuit priest Pierre Teilhard de Chardin found himself far from any church in which to celebrate the Eucharist. Instead, he created in his imagination a quite different kind of ritual: the "Mass on the World." In this prayer he makes the entire world his altar and offers as bread and wine all the vast creation that surrounds him. He begins by thanking God for "all those you have given me to sustain and charm me."

This is where the Catholic belief in the Communion of Saints begins: a grateful awareness of our own extended families: all those ancestors from whose stock we have come and the many children, nieces, and nephews who will carry on the faith; we belong together as clan and communion. From this straightforward awareness we are able to let our imaginations expand to an awareness of the millions of believers, saints and sinners, who are members of this vast

Christian communion extending over millennia. Teilhard de Chardin envisioned "before me the whole vast anonymous army of living humanity." He prays for and with "this restless multitude . . . this ocean of humanity."

He then expanded his focus to all the vast elements that make up the whole universe. In his mystic gaze this will be his cosmic Communion of Saints. He thanks God for giving him "an overwhelming sympathy for all that stirs within the dark mass of matter," and he admits that he himself is "less a child of heaven than a son of earth." [10]

In the Second Vatican Council the church celebrated this belief that Teilhard de Chardin so mystically presented. In the document on the church we read of "a pilgrim church—this communion of the whole mystical body of Jesus Christ." This transhistorical gathering is celebrated as "the living communion that exists between us and our sisters and brothers who are in the glory of heaven" (*Lumen Gentium* §51).

The Communion of Saints Today

In his award-winning essay "Late Victorians," the Catholic essayist Richard Rodriguez describes a specific gathering of Catholics that he recognizes as a Communion of Saints. This was during the era when AIDS was decimating gay lives in San Francisco and elsewhere. The parish where he was attending Mass that Sunday was honoring those volunteers who had ministered to the ill and dying in the larger community.

Rodriguez watches from a back pew this ungainly troop of Christians approaching the altar as they are summoned. "And the saints of this city have names listed in the phone book, names I heard called through a microphone one cold

Sunday in Advent as I sat in Most Holy Redeemer [parish]."
As their names are called, they come forward: "Young men
and women, and middle-aged and old, straight, gay, and all
of them shy at being called." Rodriguez fixes his gaze on a
person sitting in front of him, a man "in his seventies, frail,
his iodine-colored hair combed forward and pasted upon
his forehead. Fingers of porcelain clutched the pearly beads
of what must have been his mother's rosary." Rodriguez
recognizes "something of the old dear about him, wizened
butterfly, powdered old pouf. Certainly he is what I fear
becoming."

This individual rises and "strides into the sanctuary to
take his place in the company of the Blessed." Rodriguez
ends the essay praising these ordinary persons who got
their hands dirty caring for those dying of AIDS: "these
learned to love what is corruptible, while I, barren skeptic,
reader of Augustine, curator of the earthly paradise . . . I
shift my tailbone upon the cold, hard pew."[11]

Communities of Memory

Sociologist Robert Bellah has written of "communities of
memory." Such gatherings recount stories of their past: of
the women and men who built up and defended this particular group. These memories energize the community with
the expectation that it will endure and even thrive. "The
communities of memory that tie us to the past also turn us
toward the future as communities of hope." Our individual
lives expand and become enriched as they feel the links
with ancestors and with future generations that might carry
on our own best hopes. "People growing up in communities
of memory not only hear the stories that tell how the community came to be, what its hopes and fears are, and how

its ideals are exemplified in outstanding men and women; they also participate in the practices—ritual, aesthetic, ethical—that define the community as a way of life."[12]

Novelist Marilynne Robinson finds such a communion in the transgenerational gathering of authors. As a writer and reader of fiction, she lives among thousands of characters who do not literally exist but who people her imagination. "Community, at least community larger than the immediate family, consists very largely of imaginative love for people we do not know or whom we know very slightly." She refers to these multitudes as "the nonexistent, that great clan whose numbers increase prodigiously with every publishing season. I think fiction may be, whatever else, an exercise in the capacity for imaginative love, or sympathy, or identification."

For Robinson, this "communion" extends beyond historical figures to include the authors who inhabit her book shelves. "All together they are my community, the creators of the very idea of books, poetry, and extended narratives, and of the amazing human conversation that has taken place across millennia, through weal and woe, over the heads of interest and utility."[13]

All Saints and All Souls

A millennium ago, Christians in northern Europe believed that the year came to an end with the completion of the harvest and fading power of the sun. Celtic peoples believed that it was at this "end time" that the recently deceased were expected to complete their journey to the other world. Feasts emerged around the beginning of November that celebrated this passage of souls to God.

But at the same time, Elizabeth Johnson explains, other beliefs saw this as a time of danger, when the Lord of death sent evil spirits through the world to harass humans; tricks and treats and disguises were necessary to avoid this evil. From this tradition grew the celebration of Halloween (holy eve). The Christian church countered this darker version of the end time with the celebration of All Saints, recognizing "all the blessed dead, including family members and friends and loved ones." Instead of the terror of "moaning ghosts and evil spirits, the day celebrated the victory of Christ over evil and death."[14]

The feast of All Saints on the first day of November is the church's celebration of the Communion of Saints. Not long after this feast day was established, a growing anxiety among Christians about the suffering of their loved ones in purgatory spurred the abbot of the influential monastery at Cluny to establish the feast of All Souls on November 2, the day after All Saints' Day.

On All Saints' Day we celebrate those who have illumined the path for us believers to follow. This includes patron saints of individual locales as well as our own ancestors who have kept the faith "in spite of dungeon, fire and sword." Today we include among these saints Dorothy Day and Martin Luther King and Dietrich Bonhoeffer. On All Souls' Day we remember our more immediate families and those who have proceeded us into the next life. We revivify our relationship with these persons, living still in memory and gratitude.

In both of these religious feasts we let our individual lives rest a bit in this larger story, this greater adventure. Our little lives become caught up in the enchantment of the Communion of Saints.

Resources

1. Flannery O'Connor, "The Revelation," in *Flannery O'Connor: The Complete Stories* (New York: Farrar, Straus and Giroux, 1989), 491.

2. John Thiel explores the Communion of Saints in his *Icons of Hope: The "Last Things" in Catholic Imagination* (Notre Dame, IN: University of Notre Dame Press, 2013). See pp. 50 and 175.

3. Elizabeth Johnson, *Friends of God and Prophets: A Feminist Theological Reading of the Communion of Saints* (New York: Continuum, 1998), 2.

4. Ibid., 8.

5. Georges Bernanos, *The Diary of a Country Priest* (New York: Macmillan, 1937), 289.

6. Ibid., 260.

7. Day, *The Long Loneliness*, 139.

8. Taylor, *A Secular Age*, 751.

9. Ibid., 754.

10. Teilhard de Chardin, "Mass on the World," 145–46.

11. Richard Rodriguez, "Late Victorians," *Harper's Magazine*, October 1990, 66. This essay was reprinted in Rodriguez's *Days of Obligation* (New York: Viking Penguin, 1992).

12. Robert Bellah et al., *Habits of the Heart* (San Francisco: Harper and Row, 1985), 153, 154.

13. Marilynne Robinson, *When I Was a Child I Read Books* (New York: Farrar, Straus and Giroux, 2012), 21.

14. Johnson, *Friends of God*, 98–99.

Chapter Twelve

Enchanting Our Days:
Redeeming the Time

Be careful, then, how you live . . . redeem the time.
Ephesians 5:16

"**H**IS TROUBLE WAS with time. . . . His trouble was, he liked to refuse time." In Alice McDermott's novel *The Ninth Hour,* Jim was a young man who resisted the daily grind of rising early and showing up for work on time. He wanted to believe that his time with his wife "belonged to themselves alone, that they could do as they pleased with it." And so he would allow himself the leisure of arriving at work late or missing a day altogether, which led to his being fired, and the dire consequences that followed.[1]

Still in the first chapter of this novel we are introduced to Sister Jeanne, a member of the Little Nursing Sisters of the Sick Poor. The young nun muses on how her days unspool through four shifting moods. "Deep night frightened her beyond reason." Knowing this fear was irrational "didn't stop the terror she could brew for herself when she awoke to pray at 3:00 a.m." But once the day was begun, "the busy, crowded sunlight hours, filled with casework, hardly gave her a moment to raise her eyes." And "suppertime, ever since she had come to the convent, was a calm that God need not enter, since the bread and the soup were always good and the company of the other women, tired from a long day of nursing, was sufficient to itself." There remained a fourth experience of time that was completely different.

"For Sister Jeanne the first hour of any day, the hour of Lauds, was always the holiest. It was the hour she felt closest to God, saw Him in the gathering light, in the new air, in the stillness of the street . . . everything waking, beginning again." It seemed to her that "it was at this hour that the whole city smelled to her like the inside of a cathedral— damp stone and cold water and candle wax. . . ."[2]

When St. Paul encouraged his listeners to "redeem the time," he was asking this first generation of Christians to avoid squandering their precious days in wasteful distractions. Redeeming the time—liberating ourselves from the overwrought and over-scheduled lives we have created for ourselves—continues as a daunting task in our communities today. Time figures prominently in the Catholic imagination with its liturgical year, its matins and vespers, and its worries about eternity.

Catholic writers in the twentieth century, from T. S. Eliot to Walker Percy, have turned to the mystery of everyday time in efforts to name the disenchantment that plagues our lives. T. S. Eliot's poetic obsession with time begins in *The Waste Land*. Amid the fevered fragments of this poem we suddenly meet the plea repeated five times in capital letters: "HURRY UP PLEASE ITS TIME."[3] This request, as at a tavern's closing, announced that something was coming to an end. He was composing this poem, of course, after World War I and its fields of loss and bitter endings. How to salvage some sense of meaning and purpose when the time is out of joint?

After joining the Anglican Church Eliot came into the

legacy of its rich, religious imagery. Ash Wednesday—the inauguration of a special time in the church's liturgical year—gave him a new means to measure his wonderment about time, its ravages and possibilities. Now his concern would focus on redeeming the time—following the lead of St. Paul in his letter to the Ephesians. "Redeem/The time. Redeem/The unread vision in the higher dream" (*Ash Wednesday*).[4]

Sabbath: Enchanting Time

Our religious ancestors in ancient Israel told themselves a story about time. They knew it had to begin with the rising and setting of the sun. "And there was evening and there was morning, the first day" (Genesis 1:5). And they imagined how all the rest of creation had unfolded in God's first work week. And then a pause and a different kind of time. "So God blessed the seventh day and hallowed it, because on it God rested from all the work done in creation" (Genesis 2:3).

The creators of this story were aware there was yet another earlier story of how it all began, a sexier account of a naked couple, a garden, a snake (Genesis 2:4–3:24). But the creators of the Sabbath account had a liturgical bent, so they told of a ritual performance of creation, day after day, ending in the Sabbath where even the creator set work aside, hoping we creatures might get the point.

Our religious ancestors also recognized that even their fields needed time to rest. They declared that every seventh year they were to leave their fields fallow in order to safeguard their continued fertility (Exodus 23:11). The cardinal insight in this history was the realization that the time of our lives was malleable; it could be compressed and redirected. Its seemingly remorseless progress, from season to season, could be altered. Pauses could be inserted into otherwise long stretches of labor. Humans are not merely time's victims, bound by a 24/7 regime of production. The time of our life can be consecrated, hallowed, and redeemed.

The first generation of Christians found their time already framed by the Jewish High Holy Days. Like their ancestors they chose to honor the Sabbath, moving it forward to Sunday. Centuries later, the first Muslims likewise revered the Sabbath, moving it back to Friday. Today more than four billion persons reverence, in name if not in deed, this vision of a sacred indentation in the time of their lives.

With this temporal legacy Christians began to script their own holy days, especially those of Christmas, Easter, and Pentecost. And they added to these feasts special seasons of pause: Advent in the weeks before Christmas as a period to slow down and become attentive to the extraordinary time of Jesus's birth. And the church sought to prepare for the major celebration of Easter with forty days called Lent. After the feast of Pentecost these special periods seemed to dwindle, so liturgical leaders named the rest of the year "ordinary time" (though they must have realized that time need never be merely "ordinary").

The Scriptural Language of Time

The Christian Scriptures offered some assistance as the early generation of Christians sought to hallow time not just on the Sabbath. They found in the Bible two distinct terms for time. The word *chronos* in the Greek New Testament often describes a period of chronic suffering or constraint. When Jesus is asked to heal a person burdened by illness, he responds, "how long a time (*chronos*) has this person been sick?" (John 5:6). Such chronic time resonates with the contemporary experience of protracted illness or boredom. In another story Jesus is asked to attend to a youth who has been demonically possessed for a long period of time (*chronos*, Mark 9:2). *Chronos* here names the experience, biblical or contemporary, of obsessiveness or addiction. Both boredom (time progressing too slowly) and compulsive behavior (never enough time) qualify as *chronic* maladies. Samuel Beckett's *Godot* is the patron saint of this existential malaise.

A very different kind of time surfaces when St. Paul speaks of "redeeming the time." Here he uses the Greek word *kairos*. This term names a much more positive set of experiences. *Kairos* is the *right time* to harvest a crop before heavy rains or a frost compromises the yield. This term also names a season of special vulnerability, as when the psalmist prays, "cast me not away in the *kairos* of my old age" (Psalm 71). *Kairos* may also name a "fullness of time"— a pregnancy nearly completed or the culmination of some other important development. Mark's Gospel describes the beginning of Jesus's ministry: "The time (*kairos*) is fulfilled and the reign of God is at hand" (Mark 1:15). After months of rumination, for example, we sense the opportune moment has arrived for us to make an important decision. Attentiveness to such critical moments stands apart from both boredom and frantic activity.

Time Chronic and Unredeemed

Walker Percy, in his novel *The Moviegoer* (1961), created a character who was chronically stuck in an experience of *everydayness*—a boredom that measured the disenchanted world he inhabited. Binx Bolling has too much time on his hands and does not know what to make of it. At age twenty-nine he is earning more than enough money as a stock-broker. But he lives alone, accompanied only by a depression that he names his "malaise." Time for him unspools as an unrelieved monotony.

Binx describes his plight: "For years now I have had no friends. I spend my entire time working, making money, going to movies and seeking the company of women."[5] To stave off his chronic distress he has found two distractions: going to the movies and flirting with his serially hired sec-retaries. Neither is satisfying, but they at least lift his dark mood for the moment. Each of these diversions appears as a faux enchantment in a life that is deeply disenchanted.

Roberto Unger, in his analysis of boredom, might be commenting on Percy's novel. "Boredom is . . . the weight of unused capacity, an intimation of the freedom from which the self has hidden." In boredom, we find nothing that invites our commitment or calls for any risk. Now our only excitement will be found in what Unger defines as diversion—"the search for novelty without peril." Unger offers a precise measurement of Binx's life: "The failed life is the life that alternates between the stagnation of routinized conduct and vision and the restless craving for momentary release."[6] In such a life of unredeemed time there will be no enchantment.

Faithful to his Catholic roots, Percy situates the novel's denouement at the critical juncture of Mardi Gras and Ash Wednesday. The celebrations during the week preceding Mardi Gras, when various civic clubs (*krewes*) launch parades with flamboyant floats and people strut about in outrageous costumes, are coming to an end. These days before Ash Wednesday have been a kind of time-out-of-time, allow-ing excess before the beginning of the more sober period of Lent. The Carnival and Mardi Gras also serve for Percy as examples of a faux enchantment that, for a brief period, relieves the everydayness of life.

As Percy's novel reaches its climax, Binx and his cousin Kate leave New Orleans for Chicago, missing out on the celebrations of Mardi Gras. When they return, the party is over; it is already Ash Wednesday, and they notice people coming out of church with smudges of ash on their foreheads. This sequence in the novel is not accidental. Percy is making a point about time: the faux enchantment of Mardi Gras has been avoided and genuine change (Binx committing himself for the first time to an enduring relationship with another person) takes place in the different kind of time begun with Ash Wednesday. Lent begins and Binx's new life starts up: the superficial enchantments of movie going and brief affairs are set aside; in his commitment to Kate, time sheds its chronic quality and a richer life begins.

Walker Percy's focus on the chronic ailment of *everydayness* points to one painful experience of time: periods of boredom when nothing seems worth doing. Here we look for ways to "kill time." Percy was naming an ennui that marked the years after World War II in Europe; he had perhaps read too much Camus and Sartre as he struggled through the 1950s writing and rewriting this novel.

More typical today is the other extreme of chronically unsatisfying time: the experience of time as rushing by, vanishing before we can finish all we have signed up to accomplish. Overworking and overspending, many today find themselves in debt, deprived of sleep and out of time. A Pew Research Center survey reports: "Working parents say they are feeling stressed, tired, rushed and short on quality time with their children, friends, partners or hobbies."[7]

"Our Hearts Are Restless . . ."

Christians have inherited an inclination to restlessness. We learn that we are made for eternity and that life in this "valley of tears" should make us impatient for eternal rest. This script of restlessness comes especially from Saint Augustine. In his *Confessions,* he tells us of the unholy anxiety that marked his youthful years when his addictive desire for honors, sex, and even food drove him to a chronic restlessness. He became fearful that the charm of earthly delights might distract him from the unending beauty of God. "Our hearts are restless until they rest in thee."[8]

Augustine gave less attention to the humble restfulness that is available to us: the deep satisfaction that comes at the culmination of a worthy project, the gratifying rest with one's partner after making love; the contentment that comes as companion of well-earned fatigue.

Augustine's restlessness helped him keep his gaze on heaven, but it diminished his appreciation for creation. There can be great merit in being restless—not settling for less than the heart truly desires; there can be tragedy as well—remaining endlessly on edge, unable to commit or compromise, always looking past partial beauties and flawed humans toward an otherworldly ideal. This ideal can leave Christians suspicious of all earthly enchantments and uninterested in a world that, they have learned, is passing away (1 John 2:17).

God's Patience

The first generation of Christians lived in a culture saturated in the apocalyptic. Saint Paul seemed convinced that the end of the world was near: "We will not all die"

(1 Corinthians 15:51). The second coming of Christ could be next month, next year. One could be forgiven for being impatient for this ending of all suffering "so that God may be all in all" (1 Corinthians 15:28).

In the second half of the twentieth century a quite different vision of time and of death had begun to emerge. In a 1957 article in *Jubilee* magazine, European theologian Romano Guardini described this emerging attitude in light of "the patience of God." He reflected on God's infinite compassion in allowing the unfolding of grace in creation and in our lives. Because God has created time with its great swaths of history, "God can therefore wait until the time is ripe—the time he has himself appointed." This is a God of *kairos* who "allows things to develop quietly, freely, each thing in its own good time."[9]

John Haught, in *The New Cosmic Story*, expands on Guardini's vision of our place within a vast cosmic unfolding. Today we are familiar with the time span of the universe—matter appearing from nowhere, then morphing into living creatures, then again into consciousness as the universe became attentive to itself.[10] The natural world is more than a stage on which our eternal salvation is played out. The environment itself, abused and polluted, awaits redeeming.

Taking time seriously has some humbling aspects. We need no longer see humanity as the crown of all creation, the end-point after which there could be no more excellent creation. We are less important than we had been led to believe. Pope Francis, in his encyclical *Laudato Si'*, emphasizes our belonging to this mortal world and our responsibility for it. "As believers, we do not look at the world from without but from within, conscious of the bonds with which the Father has linked us to all things."[11] British philosopher Mary Midgely re-enforces this perspective: "We are not tourist here. . . . We are at home in this world because we are made for it. We are not fit to live anywhere else."[12]

* * * *

Art, literature, and religion all conspire to redeem the relentless flow of time, consecrating it to human purposes. Literary critic Gregory Wolfe describes his own efforts "to explore the relationship between religion, art, and culture in order to discover how the imagination might 'redeem the time.'"[13] For Wolfe, the imagination—its vitality and reach—is the clue to an appreciation of enchantment and the path toward a healing of time. Christian Wiman, in *My Bright Abyss*, joins a redeemed sense of time with hints of enchantment: "Faith cannot save you from the claims of reason, except insofar as it preserves and protects *that wonderful, terrible time* when reason, if only for a moment, lost its claim on you."[14]

Redeeming time, we rescue our everyday life from both extremes of boredom and compulsive busyness. We discover the daily disciplines that help us be truly *present*—to companions and loved ones and to ourselves. We allow God's patience to calm our self-absorbed restlessness. As we become more present to our past, this allows us to release the memories of guilt and blame we have been harboring. As we become more present to our future, we are made attentive again to hopes and ideals that we easily lose sight of in our frenetic busyness. "In patience you will possess your soul" (Luke 21:19).

Resources

1. McDermott, *The Ninth Hour,* 5 and 65.
2. Ibid., 21–22.
3. T. S. Eliot, *The Wasteland, Collected Poems,* 61.

4. Eliot, *Ash Wednesday*, in T. S. Eliot, *The Waste Land and Other Poems* (New York: Penguin, 1998), 91.

5. Walker Percy, *The Moviegoer* (New York: Random House, 1960), 41.

6. Unger, *Passion*, 112.

7. The Pew Center research quoted here is given in Claire Cain Miller's "Stressed, Tired, Rushed: Portrait of the Modern Family," *New York Times*, November 5, 2015, https://www.nytimes.com.

8. Augustine, *The Confessions*, 1.

9. Romano Guardini, "The Patience of God," *Jubilee*, May 1957, 16.

10. John Haught, *The New Cosmic Story* (New Haven, CT: Yale University Press, 2017), 77, 109.

11. *Laudato Si'*, #220.

12. Mary Midgley, *The Myths We Live By* (London: Routledge, 2004), 52.

13. Gregory Wolfe, *Beauty Will Save the World* (Wilmington, DE: Intercollegiate Studies Institute, 2011), 2.

14. Wiman, *My Bright Abyss*, 7.

Beauty Will Save the World

One thing I ask of the Lord, that will I seek after: to live in the house of the Lord all the days of my life, to gaze upon the beauty of the Lord.

Psalm 27:4

WE TRAVEL through our days minding our own business, paying our dues, meeting our obligations. Then we are confronted by something beautiful: a bird song or a blooming bush, or a puppy in full recruitment mode. "Beauty quickens. It adrenalizes. It makes the heart beat faster. It makes life more vivid, animated . . . worth living." Elaine Scarry, Harvard professor of aesthetics, then notes something yet more alarming: "it is as though one has ceased to be the hero or heroine in one's own story."[1]

When we see something beautiful—a fragile vase or a charming infant—we are recruited to its care. We are more likely to give it special attention. Here beauty elicits care; aesthetics and ethics converge.[2] The stirring of enchantment triggers a response of compassion. Theologian Sally McFague expands on this linking of beauty and care: "It is the aesthetic appreciation for the Other—God and our neighbors—that prompts the ethical response."[3] This may be the first clue that beauty might save the world.

The Beauty of Flowers

Michael Pollan, in *The Botany of Desire*, offers an enchanted history of beauty by way of the evolution of flowers. Two hundred million years ago, there were no flowers. There were ferns and mosses and conifers, but these plants lacked the fruit and large seeds that could support warm-blooded creatures. At this early stage of evolution, there was little variation or color in the world; "beauty did not yet exist."

A hundred million years ago, the world saw the emergence of angiosperms, an extraordinary class of plants that made showy flowers and formed large seeds that other species were induced to disseminate. "With flowers came fruit and seeds . . . the angiosperms multiplied the world's supply of food energy, making possible the rise of large warm-blooded mammals." His conclusion: "Without flowers we would not be."

Pollan deploys an enchanted interpretation of "desire" to mean the instinctual force that draws the bee to extract nectar from a flower and, in so doing, collect the flower's pollen to be carried to the next plant. This "desire" binds the beauty of the flower to the business of the bee. A similar "desire"—the human love of beauty—draws our attention to beautiful flowers. Such attention leads to caring for these plants, cultivating them, ensuring their survival and even flourishing. For the plant, "beauty becomes a survival strategy."[4]

And the story does not end there. Such is the fragile beauty of flowers that they have become symbols that we humans cherish. We place flowers on gravesites, at memorials after a tragedy, on the church's altar—all to celebrate the fragility and fleeting character of our own lives.

If flowers are symbolic, so are the gardens we plant and

cultivate. Pollan writes, "The garden is a place of many sacraments, an arena—at once common as any room and as
special as a church—where we can go not just to witness but
to enact in a ritual way our abiding ties to a natural world."

The garden that we create and cultivate, building
boundaries to separate it from wilderness and encroach-
ing growths, is not unlike the garden that stars in the first
book of Genesis. Such gardens are sacramental sites: we eat
the vegetables; we confess our dependence on the sun and
rain; we use some plants to heal the wasp's toxic bite. With
these gardens we "bring our abstracted upward gaze back
down to Earth for a time." Pollan's reflection concludes with
a theme similar to our own: "What a re-enchantment of the
world that would be, to look around and see that the plants
and trees of knowledge grow in the garden still."[5]

What Do Christians Make of Beauty?

Pope Francis defines the core of the gospel message—the
kerygma—as what is "most beautiful, most excellent, more
appealing and at the same time most necessary."[6] Here the
revealed truth of our religious heritage is reframed by the
pontiff as what is "most beautiful." Pope John Paul II had
earlier written, "Beauty, which in the East is one of the best
loved names expressing the divine harmony and the model
of humanity transfigured, appears everywhere: in the shape
of a church, in the sounds, in the colors, in the lights, in the
scents."[7]

A puzzle that endures in Christian history concerns the
place of beauty in this story of grace and redemption. Do
the beautiful things in the world recruit our affection, lift-
ing our sight to the Source of all loveliness? Or do beautiful
things serve more regularly to seduce and distract us from

our higher, more austere calling? Has the disenchantment of the modern world so darkened the luster of the beautiful that its sacramental power to enchant has been compromised or even erased?

In the Catholic novels we visited in Chapter 4 we saw this tension on display. In *Brideshead Revisited* Evelyn Waugh cannot conceal this suspicion of beauty: we learn that Sebastian "was magically beautiful, with that epicene quality which in extreme youth sings loud for love and withers at the first cold wind." Sebastian's sister Julia's loveliness had grown into a "haunting, magical sadness which spoke straight to the heart and struck silence; it was the completion of her beauty." [8] Fragile, human beauty is likely to soon "wither" or culminate in a shroud of sadness.

The stories of Flannery O'Connor leave little room for beauty. Her vocational focus was on the disfigured; when questioned about this predilection for the halt and the lame, she replied, "We are all grotesque!" [9] In her stories, grace is remedial, wrenching souls away from their inbuilt perversities. Perhaps the one exception is her vision of a motley crew of humans ascending toward the heavens in her rendition of the Communion of Saints—an epiphany having its own earthy enchantment.

The Christian tradition, for all its hesitance about beauty, has been dedicated in its arts, liturgical and otherwise, to beauty. The painting, sculpture, and music generated in the Medieval and Renaissance periods of Christian faith bespoke beauty as the visible face of invisible grace: the glorious beauty of Palestrina's "Ave Maria" and the tragic beauty of Michelangelo's *Pieta*; the stained glass in the cathedrals of Chartres and Notre Dame, which seizes and holds our gaze. The sumptuous liturgical ceremonies, performed with resplendently colored vestments, Gregorian chant, and pungent incense lie at the heart of the religious aesthetic of Catholic worship. The liturgy is meant to ply our senses until we are utterly enchanted.

Christ the Beautiful

"He had no form or charm to attract us, no beauty to win our hearts. He was despised, the lowest of men, a man of sorrows, familiar with suffering."
Isaiah 53:2 (Jerusalem Bible)

The crucifix, instrument of torture, leaves no room for beauty. Yet the *Pieta*, Jesus's tortured body limp on Mary's lap, is ugliness and beauty all at once. The early Christians, reading the crucified Christ into the passage in Isaiah about the suffering servant, found beauty in this poetry.

The Hebrew Scriptures point to the ambiguity that both Jews and Christians have felt about earthly beauty. In the Song of Songs the speaker describes the lover as "altogether beautiful" (6:3). "Beauty" appears seven times in this short story, but Jewish and Christian interpreters often felt the need to de-eroticize its expression and read it as symbol of God's extravagant affection for humankind. In Proverbs readers are warned that "a woman's beauty is vain" (31:30); this judgment would echo through the tradition as the abiding concern about the wiles of female loveliness.

"How beautiful on the mountain are the feet of the messenger who announces peace" (Isaiah 52:7). Saint Paul repeats this sentence (Romans 10:15), applying it to Christ. Christian art, as we have said, was dedicated both to capturing the pain of Jesus's death and the beauty of his person. Portraits in Byzantine art showed the risen Christ standing in front of the cross but now in resplendent glory. His arms are outraised not in anguish but in an embrace of the world. The triumphant Christ is most beautiful.

Poet Gerard Manley Hopkins continued this meditation on the beautiful Christ. "For Christ plays in ten thousand places/ Lovely of limbs, and lovely in eyes not his/ To the Father through the features of men's faces."[10] Still, the phrase "Christ the beautiful" will jar just a bit, since in English we tend to reserve beautiful to describe women or young children.

The New Testament story of the Transfiguration may be as close as the Scripture comes to announcing Jesus's beauty. The account expresses the astonishment of the disciples as they realize who Jesus was. How to portray such a bewildering insight? In this well-known story, told in Mark, Matthew, and Luke, Jesus and his close friends are climbing a hill. Suddenly the disciples are stunned when Jesus turns radiant. He seems to be speaking with Moses and Elijah, who had suddenly "appeared in glory" (Luke 9:31). Jesus's clothes had become all white, and he was, in a word, dazzling. The story provides much detail on the disciples' inability to process this event: they stumble and fall down; they mutter something but don't know what they are saying; they appear to be in a stupor. And then they see Jesus "in his glory." This "glory" is meant to rhyme with Moses's plea, in the Book of Exodus, to see Yahweh's glory. Glory will have to suffice as the biblical language of Christ the beautiful.[11]

The Beauty of the Gift

"Make holy these gifts." The story of our book began with this summons of the Spirit to transform bread and wine into extraordinary nourishment. Our story concludes with a return to the notion of gifts—their beauty meant to enhance their offering—and how such donations open us to an enchanted world, a reality reaching beyond the boundaries we have imposed on our lives: *what you see is what you get; you get what you deserve; life is a competition for possessions.* If a single gift is beautiful, its message opens us to another depth of beauty: a receiving and giving that is inexhaustible.

On the way to your friend's birthday dinner, you stop at a florist. From the many choices on display, you select a half-dozen beautiful lilies (not the cheaper day-old ones), pay for them, and leave the shop. Arriving at your friend's apartment, you offer her the flowers. Her eyes light up, and she breaks into a broad smile. (She does not ask how much she owes you.)

Before your purchase, the flowers were simply commodities waiting in the shop to be sold; they belonged to a market economy. With your purchase, the flowers undergo a transformation: in the alchemy of gift giving, a commodity morphs into a gift.

In the everyday world of buying and selling, we accumulate belongings and consume products. The market economy follows the law of supply and demand, with appropriate concern for profit and attention to the bottom line. This is the economy of daily life, with its dynamics of paying bills and worrying about mortgages, of insufficient wages and ever-rising costs. The market economy operates in a zero-sum world: What you spend, you lose. If you devote an hour to one activity, that hour is gone; now it cannot be used to do something else. If you spend your savings on one project, those funds are no longer available to direct elsewhere.

The market economy relies on the experience of scarcity: scarcities we find in nature and scarcities we conspire to create. It is an economy erected on the human emotion of restlessness—the unending desire for more, and the dissatisfaction with what we currently possess.

In the gift economy we are instructed in the difference between gifts and possessions. Gifts are not to be taken out of circulation or hoarded as ours alone. Instead, these gifts need to be handed on. What good is a talent for singing if no one ever hears our song? What is the point of being a gifted scholar if our knowledge is not shared with others? If we keep a gift for our private enjoyment, it begins to wither; taken out of circulation, a gift loses its vitality.

The comedian Steven Wright offers a jarring reminder of how gifts differ from possessions. In his stand-up routine he describes the array of beautiful seashells that he enjoys. Listeners picture a display case in an opulent home. Then Wright adds, "I keep them on beaches all around the world." Such beauty does not need to be taken out of circulation.

In relationships governed by the giving of gifts, we carefully remove the price tags to signal that this exchange is "not about the money." Unlike commodities, which are prudently priced to suit the market, where scarcity rules, the value of gifts points to a world of abundance. This aspect of gifts, and of an economy of the gift, turns our attention away from scarcity and alerts us to a circulation of gifts that, seen in the right light, seems endless. Lewis Hyde, in his book *The Gift*, describes this enchanting nature of the gift. "A circulation of gifts nourishes those parts of our spirit that are not entirely personal, parts that derive from nature, the group, the race, or the gods." Hyde edges toward the theme of enchantment when he observes, "We are lightened when our gifts rise from pools we cannot fathom . . . then we know they are inexhaustible."[12]

Leigh Schmidt further describes the peculiar nature of

such enchantment. "Gift practices nudge us away from the supply-side, production-oriented model of the market into the negotiable reciprocities of exchange and the uneven graces of lived experience."[13] The gift economy reminds us, again and again, that not everything can be commercialized or commodified. The most precious aspects of life—friendship, devotion, courage, compassion—resist the market mentality. Faith and fidelity are not for sale.

A society flourishes when the market economy and the gift economy are in balance. Again, Leigh Schmidt: "Dancing back and forth between products and presents, shopping and devotion . . . the gift economy . . . allows for the tiny freedoms of imagination, the modest improvisations of lived practice, and the miniature refusals of the market's power."[14] Then, career choices are enriched by a sense of vocation, and weekly paychecks are augmented by the sense of satisfaction that comes from worthwhile work. And making a living serves the larger purpose—making a life.

A World of Beauty

Dorothy Day, toward the end of her memoir, *The Long Loneliness*, recalls the judgment made by a character in Fyodor Dostoevsky's novel *The Idiot*: "Beauty will save the world."[15] For this woman, immersed up to her elbows in the unglamorous day-to-day care for the poor and marginal, beauty seemed like a surprising focus. Gregory Wolfe, in his book entitled *Beauty Will Save the World*, points to a distinctive gift of beauty: "In art, beauty takes the hard edges off truth and goodness and forces them down to earth, where they have to make sense or be revealed as imposters."[16] Annie Dillard adds her judgment: "There seems to be such a thing as beauty, a grace wholly gratuitous . . . beauty and grace are performed whether or not we will or sense them. The least we can do is try to be there."[17]

Beauty awakens us to the charm of the natural world and to the fragile loveliness of others. The dazzle of the beautiful ignites both love and care, rescuing us from an otherwise disenchanted life. At least for a moment we are rescued from ourselves and we are enchanted.

In our earthly days the beautiful is often degraded into the glamorous, even bling. Faux enchantments sparkle with promise but fail to lift our hearts or turn our affection to care for others.

Yet art and religious ritual continue to craft beautiful shapes and sounds and gestures in the desire to resonate with the Beauty that we capitalize. Finding ourselves in an environment where an exchange of gifts begins to appear inexhaustible, we may come to believe that, despite all the evidence to the contrary, beauty may save the world.

Resources

1. Scarry, *On Beauty and Being Just*, 24, 111, 113.
2. Ibid., 80.
3. Sallie MacFague, "Intimations of Transcendence, Praise and Compassion," in *Transcendence and Beyond*, ed. John Caputo and Michael Scanlon (Bloomington, IN: Indiana University Press, 2007), 151.
4. Michael Pollan, *The Botany of Desire* (New York: Random House, 2002). The quotations are from 107, xx, 109, 107, respectively.
5. Ibid., 177, 179 respectively.
6. Pope Francis, apostolic exhortation *Evangelii Gaudium* (The Joy of the Gospel), November 24, 2013, 35: Acta Apostolicae Sedis 105 (2013), 1034.
7. Pope Francis quotes his predecessor in *Laudato Si'*, §235; see Pope John Paul II's apostolic letter *Orientale Lumen* (May 2, 1995), 11; Acta Apostolicae Sedis 87 (1995), 757.

8. Waugh, *Brideshead Revisited*, 31.

9. Flannery O'Connor, *Mystery and Manners* (New York: Farrar, Straus and Giroux, 1961), 233.

10. Gerard Manley Hopkins, "As kingfishers catch fire, dragonflies draw flame," in *The Major Works*, ed. Catherine Philips (New York: Oxford University Press, 1986), 129.

11. Hans Urs von Balthasar is the Catholic theologian who spent a lifetime erecting a "theo-aesthetic" of the creator's beauty that is the origin of all created loveliness. Despite his impenetrable prose, we gain a glimpse of his work in passages such as "An apparent enthusiasm for the beautiful is mere idle talk when divorced from the sense of a divine summons to change one's life" (Aidan Nichols, *A Key to Balthasar* [Grand Rapids, MI: Baker Academic, 2011] 8, quoting von Balthasar). For a helpful introduction to von Balthasar, see Joan Roccosalvo, "Hans Urs von Balthasar—Theologian of Beauty," *The Way* 44, no. 4 (October 2005): 49–53.

12. Lewis Hyde, *The Gift: Imagination and the Erotic Life of Property* (New York: Vintage Books, 1979), 38, 20.

13. Leigh Erik Schmidt, "Practices of Exchange: From Market Culture to Gift Economy in the Interpretation of American Religion," in *Lived Religion*, ed. David Hall (Princeton, NJ: Princeton University Press, 1997), 85.

14. Ibid.

15. Day, *The Long Loneliness*, 361.

16. Gregory Wolfe, in his *Beauty Will Save the World*, recalls Aleksandr Solzhenitsyn beginning his Nobel Prize lecture with this same observation about the power of beauty. His quotation on the relation of beauty to truth appears on p. xiv.

17. Dillard, *Pilgrim at Tinker Creek*, 10.

Bibliography

Aquinas, Thomas. *Opusculum* 16, *De trinitate* 6.2, ad 5. Quoted in Margaret Miles, *Image as Insight*, 142.

Aurelius, Marcus. *Meditations*. New York: Bobbs-Merrill, 1963.

Avis, Paul. *God and the Creative Imagination*. London: Routledge, 1999.

Bellah, Robert, and Steven Tipton. *The Bellah Reader*. Durham, NC: Duke University Press, 2006.

Bellah, Robert, Richard Madsen, William Sullivan, Ann Swidler, and Steven Tipton. *Habits of the Heart: Individualism and Commitment in American Life*. San Francisco: Harper & Row, 1985.

Bardugo, Leigh. "Steeped in Enchantment: A Review of Alice Hoffman's *Nightbird*." In the *New York Times Book Review*, April 12, 2015. Online edition.

Berman, Morris. *The Re-enchantment of the World*. Ithaca, NY: Cornell University Press, 1981.

Bernanos, George. *The Diary of a Country Priest*. New York: Macmillan, 1937.

Bettelheim, Bruno. *The Uses of Enchantment: The Meaning and Importance of Fairy Tales*. New York: Vintage Books, 1977.

Bottum, Joseph. "The Things We Share." *Commonweal*. August 23, 2013. Online edition.

Brown, Peter. *Body and Society: Men, Women, and Sexual Renunciation in Early Christianity*. New York: Columbia University Press, 1988.

————. *Through the Eye of a Needle: Wealth, the Fall of Rome, and the Making of Christianity in the West, 350–550 AD*. Princeton, NJ: Princeton University Press, 2012.

Brueggemann, Walter. "Imaginative Remembering." In *An Introduction to the Old Testament*. Louisville, KY: Westminster John Knox, 2003.

————. *The Prophetic Imagination*. Philadelphia: Fortress Press, 1978.

Bynum, Caroline. *Metamorphosis and Identity*. Cambridge, MA: MIT Press, 2001.

Carson, Anne. *Eros the Bittersweet*. Princeton, NJ: Princeton University Press, 1986.

Carson, Rachel. *Silent Spring*. New York: Houghton Mifflin, 1962.

————. *The Edge of the Sea*. Boston: Houghton Mifflin, 1955.

Chang, Aloysius B. "Ch'i and some Theological Themes." *Collectanea Theologica Universitatis Fujen* 53 (1982): 341–68.

Chuang Tzu. *The Book of Chuang Tzu*. Translated by Martin Palmer. New York: Penguin, 2006.

Connelly, William. *A World of Becoming*. Durham, NC: Duke University Press, 2011.

Cooper, David. *A Philosophy of Gardens*. New York: Oxford University Press, 2006.

Cottingham, John. *The Spiritual Dimension: Religion, Philosophy and Human Value*. Cambridge: Cambridge University Press, 1995.

Crawford, Donald. "A Philosophy of Gardens." *Notre Dame Philosophical Reviews* (2007). Online edition.

D'Arcy, Martin. *The Mind and Heart of Love: Lion and Unicorn—A Study of Eros and Agape*. New York: Meridian Books, 1956.

Davenport, Guy. "Eros, His Intelligence." Pp. 135–43 in *The Hunter Gracchus*. Washington, DC: Counterpoint, 1996.

Day, Dorothy. *The Long Loneliness*. San Francisco: Harper & Row, 1952.

Dillard, Annie. *Pilgrim at Tinker Creek*. New York: Harper-Collins, 1974.

Donovan, Mary Ann. "Alive to the Glory of God." *Theological Studies* 49 (1988): 283–97.

Dupré, Louis. *Passage to Modernity: An Essay in the Hermeneutics of Nature and Culture*. New Haven, CT: Yale University Press, 1993.

Dykstra, Craig. "Pastoral and Ecclesial Imagination." In *For Life Abundant*. Edited by Dorothy Bass and Craig Dykstra. Grand Rapids, MI: Eerdmans, 2008.

Eliot, T. S. *Ash Wednesday*. In *T. S. Eliot, The Waste Land and Other Poems*. Selected and with an Introduction by Helen Vendler. New York: Penguin, 1998.

———. *The Waste Land*. New York: Norton, 2001.

Farley, Margaret. "Ethics, Ecclesiology, and the Grace of Self-Doubt." Pp. 55–75 in *A Call to Fidelity*. Edited by James Walter, Timothy O'Connell, and Thomas Shannon. Washington, DC: Georgetown University Press, 2002.

Farley, Wendy. *Eros for the Other*. University Park, PA: Penn State University Press, 1996.

———. *The Wounding and Healing of Desire*. Louisville, KY: Westminster John Knox Press, 2005.

Fingarette, Herbert. *Confucius: The Secular as Sacred*. San Francisco: HarperSanFrancisco, 1972.

Foley, Edward. *Ritual Music: Studies in Liturgical Musicology*. Collegeville, MN: Liturgical Press, 1996.

Ford, David. *Self and Salvation*. Cambridge: Cambridge University Press, 1999.

Francis, Pope. *The Francis Chronicles*. In *National Catholic Reporter* September 9, 2016. ncronline.org/blogs/francis -chronicles/Pope-Francis-new-bishops.

———. "Homily to New Bishops." ZENIT.org/articles/pope-francis-address-to-new-bishops, September 10, 2015.

———. *Laudato Si'*. Huntington, IN: Our Sunday Visitor, 2015.

Fuller, Robert. *Wonder: From Emotion to Spirituality*. Chapel Hill, NC: University of North Carolina Press, 2006.

Gooch, Brad. *Flannery: A Life of Flannery O'Connor*. New York: Little, Brown, 2009.

Gordon, Mary. *The Company of Women*. New York: Ballantine, 1980.

———. *Final Payments*. New York: Random House, 1978.

———. *Good Boys and Dead Girls and Other Essays*. New York: Viking, 1991.

Greeley, Andrew. *The Catholic Imagination*. Berkeley, CA: University of California Press, 2001.

Greene, Graham. *The End of the Affair*. New York: Penguin, 1951.

Guardini, Romano. "The Patience of God," *Jubilee*, May 1957, 16–18.

Hansen, Ron. *Marietta in Ecstasy*. New York: HarperCollins, 1991.

———. *A Stay against Confusion: Essays on Faith and Fiction*. New York: HarperCollins Perennial, 2002.

Haught, John. *The New Cosmic Story: Inside Our Awakening Universe*. New Haven, CT: Yale University Press, 2017.

Heaney, Seamus. *The Redress of Poetry*. New York: Farrar, Straus and Giroux, 1996.

Hilkert, Catherine. *Naming Grace*. New York: Continuum, 1997.

Hopkins, Gerard Manley. "God's Grandeur." In *The Major*

Works. Edited by Catherine Philips. New York: Oxford University Press, 1986.

———. "As kingfishers catch fire." In *The Major Works.* Edited by Catherine Philips. New York: Oxford University Press, 1986.

Hyde, Lewis. *The Gift: Imagination and the Erotic Life of Property.* New York: Vintage Books, 1979.

Jenkins, Richard. "Disenchantment, Enchantment and Re-Enchantment: Max Weber at the Millennium." *Max Weber Studies* 1 (2000): 11–32.

Johnson, Elizabeth. *Friends of God and Prophets: A Feminist Theological Reading of the Communion of Saints.* New York: Continuum, 1998.

King, Thomas. *Teilhard's Mass: Approaches to "The Mass on the World."* New York: Paulist Press, 2005.

Küng, Hans, and Julia Ching. *Christianity and Chinese Religion.* New York: Doubleday, 1989.

Kwong Lai Kuen. *Qi chinois et anthropologie chrétienne,* Paris: L'Harmattan, 2000.

Lahr, John. "The Laughing Cure." *New Yorker.* October 18, 2004.

———. "Trapped in Time." *New Yorker.* March 5, 2007.

Lakeland, Paul. *The Wounded Angel: Fiction and the Religious Imagination.* Collegeville, MN: Liturgical Press, 2017.

Lamott, Annie. *Small Victories.* New York: Riverhead Books (Penguin), 2014.

Lane, Anthony. "Come Back." *New Yorker.* July 10 and 17, 2017, 92.

Lepore, Jill. "The Shorebird." *New Yorker.* March 26, 2018, 64–72.

Lucas, Thomas. "Virtual Vessels, Mystical Signs." *Studies in the Spirituality of Jesuits* 35, no. 5 (November 2003): 15–45.

Maclean, Norman. *A River Runs through It.* Foreword by Annie Proulx. Chicago: University of Chicago Press, 2001.

Mariani, Paul. *God and Imagination: On Poets, Poetry, and the Ineffable.* Athens, GA: University of Georgia Press, 2002.

McDermott, Alice. *The Ninth Hour.* New York: Farrar, Straus, and Giroux, 2017.

McFague, Sallie. "Intimations of Transcendence, Praise and Compassion." Pp. 151–68 in *Transcendence and Beyond.* Edited by John Caputo and Michael Scanlon. Bloomington, IN: Indiana University Press, 2007.

Macdonald, Helen. *H Is for Hawk.* New York: Grove, 2014.

MacIntyre, Alasdair. *After Virtue.* Notre Dame, IN: University of Notre Dame Press, 1981.

Mamet, David. "Attention Must Be Paid." *New York Times,* Sunday, February 3, 2005, 13.

Mahoney, John. *The Making of Moral Theology.* Oxford: Clarendon Press, 1987.

McInerny, Ralph. *Some Catholic Writers.* South Bend, IN: St. Augustine Press, 2007.

Merton, Thomas. *Conjectures of a Guilty Bystander.* New York: Doubleday, 1968.

———. *Seeds of Contemplation.* New York: New Direction Books, 1962.

———. *The Seven Storey Mountain.* New York: Harcourt, 1948.

Mencius. Translated by D. C. Lau. New York: Penguin, 2003.

Midgley, Mary. *The Myths We Live By.* London: Routledge, 2004.

Miles, Margaret. *Image as Insight: Visual Understanding in Western Christianity and Secular Culture.* Boston: Beacon Press, 1985.

Miller, Claire Cain. "Stressed, Tired, Rushed: Portrait of the Modern Family." *New York Times.* November 5, 2015.

Mitchel, Nathan. *Real Presence*. Chicago: Liturgy Training Publications, 1998.

Neiman, Susan. *Moral Clarity*. Princeton, NJ: Princeton University Press, 2009.

Nelson, James. "Love, Power and Justice in Sexual Ethics." Pp. 288–94 in *Christian Ethics*. Edited by Lisa Cahill and James Childress. New York: Pilgrim Press, 1996.

Nussbaum, Martha. *Cultivating Humanity*. Cambridge, MA: Harvard University Press, 1997.

———. *Upheavals of Thought: The Intelligence of Emotions*. Cambridge: Cambridge University Press, 2001.

Nygren, Anders. *Agape and Eros*. Translated by William Watson. Philadelphia: Westminster Press, 1953.

O'Connor, Flannery. "Revelation." In *Flannery O'Connor: The Complete Stories*. New York: Farrar, Straus and Giroux, 1989.

O'Meara, Thomas. "A History of Grace." Pp. 76–91 in *A World of Grace*. Edited by Leo J. O'Donovan. Washington, DC: Georgetown University Press, 1995.

Oliver, Mary. *Upstream*. New York: Penguin, 2016.

Orsi, Robert. *History and Presence*. Cambridge, MA: Belknap Press, 2016.

Overbye, Dennis. "During an Eclipse: Darkness Falls, Wonder Arises." *New York Times*, August 15, 2017, D3.

Percy, Walker. *The Moviegoer*. New York: Random House, 1960.

———. *Signposts in a Strange Land*. New York: Farrar, Straus and Giroux, 1991.

Pollan, David. *The Botany of Desire*. New York: Random House, 2002.

Powers, Richard. *The Overstory*. New York: Norton, 2018.

Rahner, Karl. "Christian Humanism." Pp. 187–204 in *Theological Investigations*, vol. 9. New York: Seabury, 1976.

Ricoeur, Paul. *Figuring the Sacred*. Minneapolis, MN: Augsburg Fortress, 1995.

———. *Freud and Philosophy: An Essay in Interpretation*. New Haven, CT: Yale University Press, 1970.

———. *The Symbolism of* Evil. Boston: Beacon Press, 1963.

Robinson, Marilynne. *Days of Obligation*. New York: Viking Penguin, 1992.

———. *Gilead*. New York: Farrar, Straus and Giroux, 2001.

———. *Home*. New York: Farrar, Straus and Giroux, 2008.

———. *Housekeeping*. New York: Farrar, Straus, and Giroux. 1982.

———. *When I Was a Child I Read Books*. New York: Farrar, Straus and Giroux. 2012.

Rodriguez, Richard. "Late Victorians." *Harper's Magazine*. October 1990, 57–66.

Royal, Robert. *A Deeper Vision: Catholic Intellectual Tradition in the Twentieth Century*. San Francisco: Ignatius Press, 2015.

Saunders, George. *Lincoln in the Bardo*. New York: Random House, 2017.

Scarry, Elaine. *On Beauty and Being Just*. Princeton, NJ: Princeton University Press, 1999.

Schjeldahl, Peter. "El Greco at the Met." *New Yorker*. October 20, 2003, 198.

Schmidt, Leigh Erik. "Practices of Exchange: From Market Culture to Gift Economy in the Interpretation of American Religion." Pp. 69–91 in *Lived Religion*. Edited by David Hall. Princeton, NJ: Princeton University Press, 1997.

Schulz, Kathryn. *Being Wrong: Adventures in the Margin of Error*. New York: HarperCollins, 2010.

Schwartz, Benjamin. *China and Other Matters*. Cambridge, MA: Harvard University Press, 1996.

————. *The World of Thought in Ancient China*. Cambridge, MA: Harvard University Press, 1985.

Schweiker, William. "Understanding Moral Meanings: On Philosophical Hermeneutics and Theological Ethics." Pp. 76–92 in *Christian Ethics, Problems and Prospects*. Edited by Lisa Sowle Cahill and James F. Childress. Cleveland, OH: Pilgrim Press, 1996.

Shekleton, John. "Homosexuality and the Priesthood." *Commonweal*. November 22, 1996, 15–18.

Shweder, Richard. *Thinking Through Cultures*. Cambridge, MA: Harvard University Press, 1991.

Skelly, Michael. *The Liturgy of the World: Karl Rahner's Theology of Worship*. Collegeville, MN: Liturgical Press, 1991.

Song, C. S. *Jesus in the Power of the Spirit*. Minneapolis, MN: Fortress Press, 1994.

Sorabji, Richard. *Emotion and Peace of Mind: From Stoic Agitation to Christian Temptation*. New York: Oxford University Press, 2000.

Spohn, William. "Jesus and Christian Ethics." *Theological Studies* 56 (1995): 92–107.

Steiner, George. *Real Presences*. Chicago: University of Chicago Press, 1989.

Taylor, Charles. *A Secular Age*. Cambridge, MA: Harvard University Press, 2007.

————. "Disenchantment–Re-enchantment." In *Dilemmas and Connections*. Cambridge, MA: Harvard University Press, 2011.

Teilhard de Chardin, Pierre. *The Divine Milieu*. New York: Harper & Row, 1960.

Thiel, John. *Icons of Hope: The "Last Things" in Catholic Imagination*. Notre Dame, IN: University of Notre Dame Press, 2013.

Unger, Roberto. *Passion: An Essay on Personality*. New York: Free Press, 1984.

———. *The Self Awakened*. Cambridge, MA: Harvard University Press, 2007.

Van Norden, Brian W. "What Should Western Philosophy Learn from Chinese Philosophy?" In *Chinese Language, Thought and Culture*. Chicago: Open Court, 1996.

Vermander, Benoit. "Theologizing in the Chinese Context." *Studia Misssionalia* 45 (1996): 120–34.

Waldmeir, John. *Cathedrals of Bone: The Role of the Body in Contemporary Catholic Literature*. New York: Fordham University Press, 2009.

Waugh, Evelyn. *Brideshead Revisited*. New York: Little, Brown, 1944.

Whitehead, James, and Evelyn Whitehead. *Holy Eros: Pathways to a Passionate God*. Maryknoll, NY: Orbis Books, 2009.

———. *Nourishing the Spirit: The Healing Emotions of Wonder, Joy, Compassion and Hope*. Maryknoll, NY: Orbis Books, 2012.

Wills, Garry. *The Future of the Catholic Church with Pope Francis*. New York: Viking, 2015.

Wilson, Edward O. *Consilience: The Unity of Knowledge*. New York: Knopf, 1998.

Wiman, Christian. *My Bright Abyss: Meditations of a Modern Believer*. New York: Farrar, Straus and Giroux, 2013.

Wolfe, Gregory. *Beauty Will Save the World: Recovering the Human in an Ideological Age*. Wilmington, DE: Intercollegiate Studies Institute, 2011.

Yearley, Lee. "Ethics of Bewilderment." *Journal of Religious Ethics* 38 (2010): 436–60.

———. *Mencius and Aquinas: Theories of Virtue and Conceptions of Courage*. Albany, NY: State University of New York Press, 1990.

Index